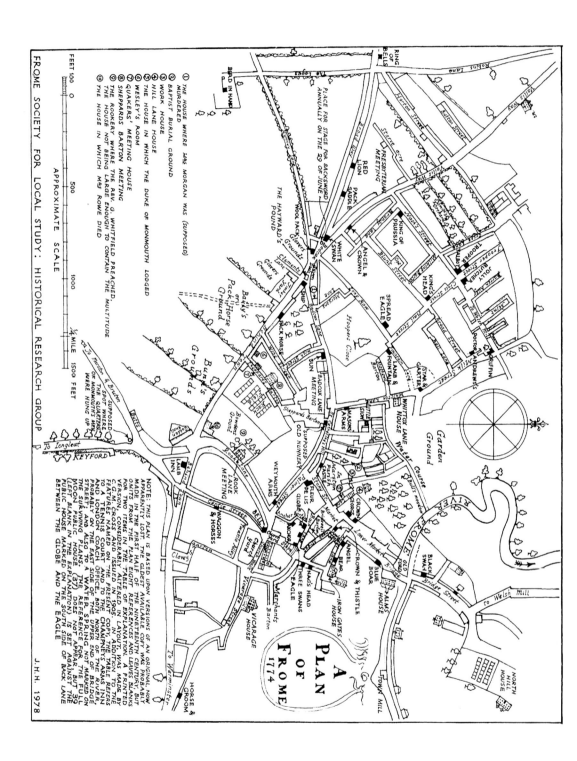

THE BOOK OF FROME

St Peter's Church, Lithograph by R. Pocock 'to the Rev[d] Charles Phillott M.A. Vicar of Frome Selwood' in the possession of the author.

A new altar-piece depicting St Peter was installed in the chancel in 1762 and the church was known as St. Peter's until the middle of the 19th century when the name reverted to St John the Baptist.

Cheap Street by W W Wheatley in 1845 (FSLS)

THE BOOK OF FROME

A HISTORY

BY

MICHAEL McGARVIE FSA

FROME SOCIETY FOR LOCAL STUDY

MMXIII

PUBLISHED BY

THE FROME SOCIETY FOR LOCAL STUDY

FIFTH EDITION 2013

PRINTED BY

BUTLER TANNER AND DENNIS

FROME

ISBN 9780956586971

Contents

Acknowledgements

I owe much gratitude to Dr John Harvey, not only for all the new material appertaining to the history of Frome which he has gathered and generously placed at my disposal, but also for stimulating discussions over the years on local historical problems, which have been worth many volumes. I have also to thank him for writing the foreword and for reading the text, although he must not be held responsible for my opinions or errors. I am also deeply in the debt of the late J.O. Lewis, whose industrious and patient work did so much to reveal Frome's past. Through the courtesy of his son and daughter, J. W. Lewis and Mrs E.J. Edmunds, I have had access to his papers and collections, in particular the typescript of his History of Frome which, regrettably, has never been published. I am grateful to Arthur Duckworth Esquire, of Orchardleigh Park, for writing the preface and for the access he has given me to his muniments and to his grandfather's remarkable diary. N.F. Maggs placed at my disposal many items of historical interest.

Mrs Hilda Massey, of Frome Museum, has allowed me to reproduce many photographs from the museum collections, and has helped me with historical information through many years. I thank her and the museum's trustees. L.V. Bowring, Chairman of the Frome Society for Local Study, and Mrs Bowring gave constant encouragement and help. I have taken full advantage of the material gathered by the Frome Historical Research Group since it started work in 1977 and am grateful to its members. Many people, some anonymous, have sent me old photographs, postcards and press cuttings. Several photographers, among them Clive Baker, Trevor Barker, Peter Lowry and Ian Mackay, have taken or copied photographs for me. The Society of Antiquaries of London, the Somerset Archaeological Society, and the Boodle Collection at Bath Reference Library have kindly allowed me to reproduce prints from their collections. Mr Thomas, of Winscombe, has allowed me to use several of the photographs he took in Frome in the mid-1950s, notably those of Keyford Hospital.

No work of this kind could be accomplished without the help of David Bromwich, the Local History Librarian at Taunton Castle, or D.M.M. Shorrocks, and his staff at the County Record Office. I am deeply beholden to them. Over a long period of research, information has been gathered here and there from many individuals and I hope they will accept a general expression of my thanks. Lastly, I must thank Mrs J.H. Willbourn who at short notice typed my manuscript and transmuted my hieroglyphics into pristine pages of print.

Foreword

by Dr John Harvey, FSA, FRSL

Frome is unusual among English towns, first by its physical setting on steep slopes and markedly different levels; but even more by its historic development. Though a place of unusual economic importance for at least seven centuries, it never achieved incorporation but remained a country parish divided between several manorial ownerships. At the Census of 1831, the last before Reform, the population was 12,240, the largest after Bath in the whole county; over a thousand greater than Taunton, and almost as big as Bridgwater and Wells put together. Frome was, moreover, the greatest of all the cloth towns of the West, substantially more populous than Bradford-on-Avon, Trowbridge or Westbury; half as big again as Stroud, and surpassing even the county-town cities of Gloucester and Salisbury. In spite of this major rank, there are no town records earlier than the late 19th century, and most of Frome's history is exceedingly hard to unravel.

Michael McGarvie has mastered the complex documentation which does survive, scattered in many repositories and in private hands, and from a multitude of facts and names has distilled an eminently readable book, both informative and entertaining. He has also succeeded in collecting a remarkable body of illustrations, many of which show how much has been lost in quite recent years, for lack of any adequate planning policy, before the designation of a substantial Conservation Area in 1976, since recognised by the Department of the Environment as of Outstanding National Importance.

Although my own family roots strike deep into the soil of East Somerset, my connection with Frome itself is tenuous and recent. I feel all the more honoured, therefore, to have been asked to write a foreword to this notable work, which on every count deserves to be an outstanding success.

Preface to the Fifth Edition

by Alastair MacLeay

Frome has been most fortunate in her amateur historians, starting with Rev WE Daniel in the 19th century and followed by JO Lewis, Peter Belham, Rodney Goodall and Derek Gill in the 20th century, but it is Michael McGarvie, who has written the first professional history of the town with the publication of 'The Book of Frome' in 1980. He has told the full fascinating story, from its founding by St Aldhelm in 685 AD until the millennium in 2000. It has been meticulously studied and entertainingly explained. Michael had planned to rewrite the final chapter to bring the book up to date, but, sadly, personal circumstances have not permitted him to do so.

This is a great pity since Frome has taken on a new lease of life. The Frome Festival, instigated by Martin Bax over ten years ago, has attracted national and international musicians, artists, authors, raconteurs, comedians and many more to create a new audience to the town's attractions. After many years of decline, Catherine Hill has been rejuvenated with new specialist shops; there is a regular monthly market on Sundays and the town has become a centre for the arts.

After three years out of print, the Frome Society for Local Study is delighted to republish this new edition by its President, so that residents of Frome, both new and old, may learn details of the town's economic and social history and gain an appreciation of the development of its remarkable ecclesiastic and vernacular architecture. Even after the destruction of half the Trinity area during the 1960s, Frome has one of the finest examples of early industrial housing in Western Europe and, for its size, the broadest cross section of non-conformist chapels in the West Country, even though many of them have now been converted to alternative uses.

Vallis Vale

And thou, sweet Vale, can'st witness bring,
From the bright days of laughing Spring,
Till Autumn yields the shorten'd day,
To ruthless Winter's awful sway; That be
their stations what they will,
Mortals love rural pleasures still.
For oft as Monday noon rolls round,
When Sol has dried the teeming ground,
What groups come trooping down the hill,
Beside the farm, or round the mill;
Regardless of the wheel and loom,
And all the cares of busy Frome:
Leaving its profits and its noise,
To seek at Vallis calmer joys.
And now the gypsying parties spread,
Some on the rocks high over head,
Some nestling snugly half-way down,
Though shapeless crags above them frown:
While some contented with the vale,
Swell the loud song, or join the tale:
Nor is the frothing jug forgot,
While visiting this favourite spot.

      *   *   *

Now all is still, save when the crash
Of rifted crag with thundering dash,
From its huge bed of limestone flung,
Echoes tremendously and long.
And not a sound beside is heard,
But bleating flock or lowing herd;
Yct who can say what deeds untold,
May here have been perform'd of old.
What joys have rapt the spirit here;
What sorrows wrung the bitter tear;
What spirits of ethereal race,
Here found their mortal dwelling place;
Panting for honourable fame,
Yet doom'd to penury and shame.

Mrs Tuck

Origins

If Austria did not exist, opined the 19th century German statesman Bismarck, speaking of the multinational empire of the Habsburgs, it would be necessary to invent her. It is unlikely that anyone would invent Frome if this distinctive town had not already existed for nearly 1300 years. It occupies a position which in its virgin state was a stony and inhospitable hillside, facing north and sloping steeply down to a marshy plain—the present Market Place—bounded by a sluggish stream and, before the mills interfered with the natural flow of the water with their weirs and sluices, subject to frequent and severe flooding. The site of the future town was on the edge of a vast tract of woodland known to the native British as coit mawr, the great wood, but later renamed by their Saxon, or English, conquerors, Selwood, Seal wuda, from the number of willows which grew in its swampy depths. On the high ground within its recesses lived backward tribes who preferred these heights to the damp and timber-choked valleys. The Selwood ridge which divided Somerset from Wiltshire gave birth to several rivers including the Wylie, the Stour and the Brue.

A lesser stream seeped out of the ground in a remote coppice later called Canwood (below Canwood Farm in the present parish of Brewham). The ancient British, to whom water was especially sacred, called it *From*, a form of the place-name recorded as early as 701. The word is said to be derived from a Welsh adjective, *ffraw*, meaning fair, fine, or brisk, but none of these attributes apply at all obviously to this modest little river and the meaning is probably little more than running water. In 1851, Thomas Bunn, a notable Frome worthy, wrote of the beginnings of the river: 'The source rises in a recess crowned with flowers, about nine miles from Frome. Few of the inhabitants of the town have seen it. Most of them would as soon think of exploring the sources of the Nile', a remark which may still hold good today. Be this as it may, the infant Frome meandered down through what was to become the Vale of Witham, was kept on a north-easterly course by the Marston ridge, but at last, finding a weak spot, (near what was to become Wallbridge) turned north-west and cut a leisurely serpentine course between North Hill and the end of the Marston ridge on which the future town of Frome was to rise. At Spring Gardens the river wore away the soft red sandstone to create a considerable plain and a notable ford. This the Saxons, who were not remarkable for imagination where place-names were concerned, called factually, 'the broad ford'. The ford was later replaced by a bridge and as Bradford Bridge the name has come down to our own day. From this point the Frome flows on beyond our immediate concern eventually to join the Avon at Freshford.

The existence of the broad ford underlines the point that ancient England was not a pathless wilderness. The Britons were considerable traders, farmers and breeders of cattle. A network of trackways facilitated travel. One of the chief routes, the Harrow way, which went from Kent to Cornwall, passed within a few miles of the town, coming off the Wiltshire downs and along the Selwood ridge through Kilmington on its way to the far West. Another track from the West came up through Bruton to Upton Noble where even a thousand years ago it is described in a Saxon charter as 'the olden wei'. It continued along the ridge towards Frome where the hamlet of Ridgeway commemorates it. A 13th century charter calls it La Rigweye. The Ridgeway divided at Gorehedge, a minor track continuing down the hill to a ford near where Frome Bridge now stands, while the main routes continued along the line of

Christchurch Street, one-south-east via Timbers Hill and Whitbourne towards Warminster, the other north-west along Christchurch Street West and Hangman's (Vernal) Lane to cross the 'broad ford' at Spring Gardens. The south-easterly route was known in 1270 as the Portway, a common name for a route between market towns and this clings to the Frome end today. However, the 'broad ford' was the easy and natural place to cross the Frome. Here the Old Way converged with the ridgeway which came down from the Mendips via Leigh and Whatley and once across, fanned out up-country towards Wellow, east towards Salisbury Plain through Chapmanslade, and into North Wiltshire, crossing the Frome again at Oldford.

The hillside above the Frome has, then, long been the haunt of men. But it is probable that the earliest inhabitants of the vicinity chose the opposite height, later known as North Hill, for their home. Here in 1820 during landscaping operations in the garden of Fromefield House, home of the great clothier family of Sheppard, a megalithic, or stone-built, tomb was discovered and recorded in a somewhat cursory way by a daughter of the house. It appears to have been a long barrow of the neolithic period—four to six thousand years old, similar to those at West Kennet or Stony Littleton, only smaller. It contained five chambers and a quantity of bones and pottery. Like a family vault in a Christian church, it may have been used for the disposal of the dead for generations. The Sheppards alas, treated the barrow with scant respect, levelling the mound and using some of the stones to build a grotto or summerhouse. The bones, however, were left undisturbed and a five foot sarsen stone which had partially covered the burial chambers was set up to mark the spot. So matters rested until 1965 when the Sheppards had passed from the scene, Fromefield House had been turned into flats and the garden given over to building development. Before the site was finally lost, it was excavated by Mr and Mrs Vatcher on behalf of the Ministry of Public Buildings and Works. The barrow was found to contain 15 burials: eight adults, four youths, a child and two infants. A singular feature was the lack of skulls and long bones thought to have been removed for ritual purposes. Little could be gleaned from the remains other than that these early inhabitants of Frome had good teeth, but tended to be arthritic. The original standing stone was unfortunately lost.

St George Gray, the long serving secretary of the Somerset Archaeological Society, suspected the existence of a complete stone circle, probably used for religious purposes, at Fromefield. Certainly, many sarsen stones have been recorded in the area and about the town. A group of stones existed where Stonelands now stands and some are said to be buried under the house. One which lay at the entrance was, according to local tradition, broken up and taken to mend the road, a common fate for barrows and stone circles. Further stones stood opposite the Bath Road entrance to Fromefield House. A sarsen is still to be seen built into the wall of the caretaker's cottage at Vallis Road Cemetery and another has been recorded near the old gas works at Welshmill. Other barrows in the vicinity remind us of these early inhabitants of the district, notably 'Big Tree' on Buckland Down, now only a slight rise in a field beside the A362, and the Murtry cromlech at Orchardleigh. Big Tree remained of special significance into the 18th century as the meeting place of the Hundred, or administrative district of Frome,and the site of the Sheriff of Somerset's tourn or court. John Strachey, Fellow of the Royal Society, who compiled notes for an unpublished history of Somerset early in the 18th century, has recorded how the Murtry cromlech, or the mound which then covered it, was made of small stones but turfed over. 'Some years agoe viz. about 1724 or 1725 taking away several loads to mend ye highway the Workmen discovered the body of a large man and several skulls lying in a sort of chest...some say a great no. of Bones.'

Apart from Fromefield and Orchardleigh Down, the centre of early population comprised the three fortresses of Tedbury, Wadbury and Newbury in the parishes of Elm and Mells. Tedbury 'the greatest and strongest of ye 3' as Strachey records, is in an impregnable position between the Mells and Fordbury streams. A fine quern for grinding corn was discovered here (it is now in Frome Museum) and pieces of several others have been found in a rockery at neighbouring Elm. Wadbury is also immensely strong, on a cliff above the Mells stream, and Newbury stands on high ground opposite them, the three lying, as Strachey points out, 'almost in an Equilateral triangle from each other'. Below Tedbury is Murdercombe, a name which has always intrigued Frome people. It is so-called in the Saxon charter of the boundaries of Mells a thousand years ago. Strachey picked up an old tradition which he records with characteristic vigour, 'that 2 Kings had a Battle, the one being possessed of ye hill, I presume Tedbury, made a great slaughter of ye other in Murders Bottom... rolling stones upon them & hanged ye prisoners live in Hangmans Lane where they brought ye Stones and heaped them one ye ded in ye westfeild (Murtry) Barrow'. Strachey was quite carried away by the idea and embroiders it with his own observations. Tedbury does not appear in mediaeval records. This is because it is disguised as Hyerburg or Higherburgh. In 1271 it was held by Osbert Giffard who granted it with other property in Elm, or Teaumes as the scribes called it, to the Branch family so that it was held to be part of the Manor of Frome. Another place where people congregated was Roddenbury Camp, close to Longleat, an important and impressive Iron Age fortress now much obscured by trees. Four hundred yards below it on Cole Hill is the curious little entrenched motte of Hales Castle, long thought to be an outpost of Roddenbury, but perhaps of Norman origin. It takes the name from Richard Hales who in 1697 leased a house which he had recently built 'on a place... called Roddenbury Hill betweene the two castles, the great castle on the Southside and the little castle on the Northside...'.

The strength of the local economy at the end of this period is faintly reflected in the Nunney hoard, a collection of 10 gold, 232 silver and four brass coins discovered by two men ploughing in a field called Eleven Acres on West Down Farm in 1860. The coins lay in a small urn under a yew tree. Sixteen of them bore the inscription Anted with a head on the obverse and a three-tailed horse on the reverse side. Another had a fern-leaf design and was inscribed Comux. Were Antedrigus and Comux local rulers who lorded it over the Frome district, until the even tenor of their ways was shattered by the Roman invasion and occupation from AD43 onwards? We cannot certainly know, but it is significant that among the native coinage is a coin of the Roman Emperor Claudius, dated AD41. The Romans secured the lucrative lead mines at Charterhouse-on-Mendip at an early date after the conquest and the Nunney hoard may well represent the wealth of a local nobleman hidden from the advancing legions and never reclaimed. One of the coins is in the County Museum at Taunton.

It is likely that by AD49 the Frome area was occupied by the military, behind whom came a mass of prospectors and speculators. Within six years of the conquest, Mendip lead was on its way to Rome, the legions making use of a British trackway which led from the Mendips to the site on Southampton Water of the Roman port of Clausentum. The lead road was a busy one and probably many inns and settlements were built in its vicinity. The exact course of the lead road south of Frome has not been determined by excavation, but it is thought that it crossed the Vale of Witham near Quarr Hill Farm and passed over Gare Hill into Wiltshire. On the north side of Barrow Wood in the parish of Witham Friary is a fine agger, or bank, which might repay investigation, being on the parish boundary and approximately on the site of a mediaeval road, known as the Hachweie, mentioned in the foundation charter of Witham Priory in 1182. In 1867 a man called Charles Strickland, draining a field on Quarr Hill Farm (the exact site is not recorded), found 110 Roman coins about a foot beneath the surface under a flat stone. At a deeper level some Roman ware was discovered. The author has found Roman pottery including Samian ware, concentrated in an area of about an acre on Great Westbarn Farm, Witham Friary. A villa at St Algar's Farm within the old parish of Frome has been partially excavated by Graham Thomas and disgorged masses of Samian, the better sort of

Roman tableware, as well as New Forest Ware and local pottery. This is close to the lead road and may have been one of the hostelries which served it.

With the rise of Bath as a great city and watering place, it is likely that the area to the south became thickly settled. Communications with the south were eased by the building of the Roman road from Poole to Bath which came up from Badbury Rings. Its course past Frome is uncertain and controversial, but it is probable that it took a natural route through the marshes by Friggle Street, possibly a direct derivation from the Roman *strada*, a metalled or paved track, already known by this name ('Friling stret') as early as 1231. It may then have continued by Rodden to cross the Frome at Oldford, passing over the Henhambridge Brook to Woolverton, where definite traces have been found on the ground. In 1930, when the foundations of a house were excavated at Styles Hill, close to this route, fragments of Roman pottery were found. More local Roman sites may await discovery, judging by the number John Prescott has found to the north of Frome in Beckington, Norton St Philip and other places.

If the Romans actually lived on the site of Frome they, like their predecessors, appear to have preferred North Hill for it was here, on the apex where the Bath and Westbury roads divide, that a Romano-British burial was discovered in 1931 during road widening. The skeleton was damaged and some of the bones lost before it could be examined. This early 'Froman' turned out to be a strongly-built man, 5 ft 9 ins tall, with a long, narrow head. He had lived on well-cooked food which had played havoc with his teeth. The skeleton was lying face downwards which hardly sounds like a regular burial. Something more formal may be suggested by the stone coffin, said to be Roman, which was discovered when Fromefield House was built in 1797. The Sheppard family, having destroyed a barrow, gave little heed to a coffin, and for many years it lay by the roadside near the house giving rise to the name Coffin Spring Lane (now Spring Road),which first appears officially in 1813. Strachey records the discovery at Tedbury in 1690 of 'a considerable quantity of Roman Coyn all brass and mostly of Constantine junior' as well as '2 arrow heads of brass copper and ye sockat for ye Plume of an helmet'.

The grandest memorial of the Roman presence near Frome is the Whatley villa, in fact in the parish of Nunney. It was discovered by some men digging a hole for a post in a field called Chessil at the end of Whiteway Lane in 1837. The local landowner, Mr Shore, of Whatley House, took an interest and excavated the site, finding a hypocaust, the under floor heating chamber for the bath, and a fine mosaic pavement. Mr Shore built a curiously shaped stone shed, the ruins of which still remain, to protect the pavement. This was erected on Roman foundations and incorporated some original stonework in herring-bone pattern. Visitors and souvenir hunters steadily eroded the pavement which remained open to view well into the present century. It was finally destroyed when a herd of cows broke into the shed. What remains has sought once again the protective mantle of the earth.

Fortunately, the interest aroused locally by the discovery—it was visited by Rev John Skinner, the antiquary of Camerton, among other local notables—ensured that some record was made. Mr Shore commissioned one John Hill to make a coloured drawing of the floor, while Joseph Chapman, a Frome sculptor, chiselled a model of the bath suite out of stone. This, too, is now in Frome Museum. The mosaic, which was in seven colours and covered the floor of two inter-connecting rooms, including the *triclinium*, or dining-room, was visited in 1864 by W.J. Harvey, a Frome journalist, who left a description in the Marston Bigot Parish Magazine, then a publication with literary pretensions under the influence of Mrs Richard Boyle, wife of the Rector and well-known to the Victorians under the *nom-de-plume* of E.V.B. (Eleanor Vere Boyle).

Harvey records a head of Cybele, holding a sceptre and made of black and red tile and limestone, 'an elephant carefully and accurately represented', and a hunting leopard springing on a stag. He was told that the central picture represented Orpheus taming the wild beasts by the music of his lyre, a common enough theme for such a pavement. It had already been largely destroyed. In the apse was a representation of a dolphin 'in a very delapidated and forlorn condition'. All that Harvey saw is faithfully rendered in Hill's sketch.

In recent years the Villa has been excavated by the Inspectorate of Ancient Monuments and by the Frome Society for Local Study. Among the finds were the skeletons of three children. Archaeologists believe that the villa was built about 300 AD and largely destroyed about 50 years later. There is a field called Chesix on Postlebury Hill, Cloford, where Rev John Collinson, historian of Somerset, recorded the tradition of a Roman villa and a find of coins. It is itself too steep sided to be the site of any dwelling, but may reflect that there was one close by. Chessil and Chesix may well derive from old English *ceasel* often indicating the remains of a Roman villa.

The Roman connection with Frome is in the nature of a will-o'-the-wisp. The presence of Rome is all around but defies definition or capture. The Romans, like the Britons before them, seem to have turned their backs on the northern end of the Marston ridge when looking for a place to settle and to have chosen instead more sheltered and salubrious spots in the neighbourhood.

Bradford Bridge, Spring Gardens, stands on the old Broad Ford, where the river crossing the old red sandstone was wide and shallow. The river bed has been lowered to allow flood water to drain away from the town, leaving the bridge on stilts. (FM)

15

ABOVE:Ancient tracks: a section of the coach road from Salisbury to Bath, near Oldford, and Coalway Lane. (FM) BELOW: The embankment at Roddenbury Camp; a photograph taken before the trees grew up. (FM)

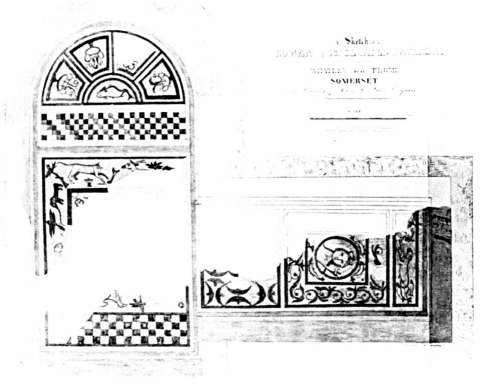

ABOVE LEFT: Henham Bridge, a later construction on the line of the Roman road from Poole to Bath. (FM) RIGHT: Miss Eunice Overend, of the Frome Society for Local Study, excavating part of the water supply of the Whatley Roman villa. (FM) BELOW: John Hill's sketch of the Roman pavement at Whatley. (SAS)

ABOVE LEFT: St Aldhelm, holding a model of one of his monasteries, from a statue by J. Forsyth in St John's Church, c1865. (JWL) RIGHT; Gentle Street, formerly Hunger Lane, one of the Saxon thoroughfares of Frome, c1900. CENTRE: Malmesbury Abbey, the great mediaeval foundation which rose on the site of the monastery of St Aldhelm. BELOW: Saxon stones in the tower of St John's, possibly part of a memorial cross to St Aldhelm. (CB)

Saints and Sinners

Of Frome between the departure of the Romans in AD 410 and the coming of St Aldhelm, the apostle of Wessex, about the year 685, there is little information. The gradual collapse of Britannia into warring fragments was given the evocative, if not strictly accurate, name of The Dark Ages. The Romans gave way to a British High King Vortigern who, to contend with the depradations of the Picts and Scots, called in English and Saxon mercenaries from Germany. So Hengist and Horsa broke into national history. The long and successful fight back by the British under Arthur, traditionally associated with South Cadbury Castle within 20 miles of Frome, caught the imagination of Europe and secured an undying place in world literature. But it only postponed the establishment of Saxon rule.

In Somerset the Roman system probably decayed gently, staggering on a generation or two. By the middle of the sixth century the bitter fighting between the West Saxons, whose Kingdom was centred on Wiltshire, and the Britons of Dumnonia, as the West of England was called, had destroyed the vestiges of Romano-British civilisation and led to anarchy in the no-man's-land between the two nations. Bath became a border town and suffered cruelly as a result.

The tide of English conquest moved inexorably on. In 577 the Saxon leaders Cuthwine and Ceawlin inflicted a crushing defeat on the Britons at Dyrham and occupied Bath, Gloucester and Cirencester. Englishcombe, the valley of the English, outside Bath, probably commemorates this conquest and settlement. It was not until 658, however, that their successor, Kenwalh, finally occupied central Somerset and established his frontier at the River Parrett. The decisive battle was fought within 10 miles of Frome at Penselwood, a natural fortress then known merely by its British name of Pen, meaning a hill. As late as the 19th century the earthwork fortification on top of the Pen ridge here on the borders of Somerset and Wiltshire was known to the woodmen as Kenniwilkins Castle, the name perhaps enshrining some dim folk memory of the Saxon King and his victory. Henceforth the English conquest stood and the Frome area lay open for settlement by the victors, although H. M. Porter, the historian of the conquest of Somerset and Devon, who, incidentally was born at Frome, has suggested that the Battle of Posentesbyrig, fought in 661 and usually identified with Posbury in Devon or Pontesbury in Shropshire, may represent a counter-attack by the Britons. In this case, the engagement may have been fought at Postlebury, a prominent hill in the parish of Cloford, a couple of miles south-west of Frome. The name appears to be derived from 'post burg', (it is Postbury in 1182), perhaps indicating that the hill top was defended by the palisade of stakes, although local people say that an apostle is buried there, a pleasant example of folk etymology.

Whatever the result of the Battle of Postlebury, if such there was, it did little to alter the facts of the English conquest. The spoils gained by the Battle of Pen were not to be given up. Those spoils are reflected in the place-names surrounding Frome which amount to a roll call of the Saxons who settled in the area: Nunney, Nunna's island; Wanstrow, Waendel's tree; Kilmington, Cynehelm's farm; Witham, Wita's homestead, and many others, although this may have been a long and gradual process facilitated by marriage as well as conquest. The early hatred between the two races is recorded simply, but graphically, by Matthew of Westminster who noted that the Britons would 'take no ransom for an English captive save his head'.

The Saxons and English had been pagans but with the coming of St Augustine and his Roman missionaries to Canterbury in 597 were rapidly converted to Christianity. Once they had accepted the new faith, the Saxon royal families could not contain their enthusiasm and vied with each other in piety and proselytising. The Royal Family of what we may now call Wessex was second to none in zeal and about the year 639 brought forth, probably at Wareham in Dorset, Aldhelm, later to be canonised, to become an ornament of faith and learning, and the founder of Frome as we know it.

Aldhelm was much subjected to authors, as the Duke of Wellington would have said, five lives being written of him, two of which survive, one by William of Malmesbury, generally a sound and painstaking historian, and the other by Faricius, Abbot of Abingdon. According to William, Aldhelm was the son of Kenten, a distant relative of Ine, the great King of Wessex (688-726). He was educated by Maidulf, a learned Irish monk, studying Latin verse, Roman law, astrology, astronomy and arithmetic as well as the scriptures in which he became exceptionally well-read. He improved himself by travel in France and Italy before acquiring a final polish from St Adrian at Canterbury 'the most learned professor of the sciences who had ever been in England'. About the year 661 he joined his former tutor, Maidulf, in his cell in the Forest of Braden in Wiltshire at a place which came to be called Malmesbury, possibly a compromise between Mai- or Maldulfesbury and Aldhelmsbury. At Malmesbury Aldhelm's light was by no means buried under a bushel. His fame as a scholar spread not only through England but also overseas and eclipsed that of his teachers.

In 675, Maidulf died and Aldhelm became Abbot of the monastery which had grown up at Malmesbury. Here scholars came from as far afield as France and Scotland to study under him. Although he never deserted the acquisition of knowledge, his thoughts turned more and more to missionary work. For the next 30 years he was constantly on the move preaching and exhorting in the forest areas of Braden and Selwood. Aldhelm was well suited to his task, at 35 in the prime of life, a man of strength and stamina well suited to constant journeys along execrable roads. In William of Malmesbury's time his chasuble was still preserved and proved him to be a big man. He had other attributes, which made him peculiarly fitted for evangelical work, not least of which was that he possessed the common touch. King Alfred, who preserved much of this work in a Handbook, now alas lost, considered him the best of the English poets.

Aldhelm's job was not so much to convert the heathen, although there may have been pockets of these living in remote parts of Selwood, but to reconcile the Celtic Christianity of Somerset with the Roman norm as introduced to Kent by St Augustine. The Celtic Church was not considered Orthodox by Rome, the chief bone of contention being that they celebrated Easter at the wrong time. Aldhelm wrote a notable and influential book against this error. Another cause of dispute seems to have been that the Celts rejected the circular tonsure worn by the Roman clergy. Aldhelm's efforts were successful and he was able to convert the native population to the Roman practice. He was ahead of his time in his wish for reconciliation and conversion by reason rather than by force.

In 676, Osric, King of Mercia, built a church at Bath and this may have stimulated Aldhelm to found churches himself. His name is associated with the Saxon church of St Laurence at Bradford-on-Avon, a now vanished church of St Peter at Bruton, and churches at Sherborne, Doulting and at Wareham on his Dorset estates, near which St Aldhelm's Head commemorates him. Traditionally, he is also associated with Godminster outside Bruton. Bruton appears to have been a great centre of religious activity, for William of Malmesbury writes that on his return from a pilgrimage to Rome, Aldhelm brought with him a small marble altar slab for Ine, which the King gave to a church he had founded at Bruton in honour of the Virgin Mary.

Sometime before his visit to Rome in 688 (if indeed the visit is not an invention of his biographers) Aldhelm decided to establish a mission to the heathen or misguided Celtic Christians in the middle of Selwood, so as to be closer to the tribes which inhabited the area. So was founded the Church of St John, the Baptist at Frome. The dedication was probably an allusion to the fact that St John had also preached in the wilderness. Faricius tells of its foundation tersely enough, in that Aldhelm applied to Pope Sergius that the monastery at Malmesbury 'and another he built in honour of St John, on the river which is called Froom, might be rendered free from all secular service'. This is confirmed by William of Malmesbury writing in 1125, when St Aldhelm's Church still survived. A Papal bull of 701 confirmed the privileges of Malmesbury and Frome and is our first documentary reference to the town.

The foundation of the church had a profound influence on the development of Frome, which grew up in its shadow. Aldhelm's choice of site on the north end of the Marston ridge is remarkable. We cannot be sure of his reasons. Almost certainly the main factor was the fresh springs which rose on the slope, referred to by Leland in 1540 as 'a right fair spring in the churchyard that by pipes and trenches is conveyed to divers parts of the town'. Thomas Bunn in 1851 makes sardonic mention of the 'fine spring flowing through the churchyard ... among coffins and skeletons ... he had heard that it was good to have body in wine, but he had never heard that it was desirable in water'. Today, the spring which gladdened Aldhelm's eye still flows to feed the fountain and the leat in Cheap Street. The spring not only provided a fresh water supply to the new monastery but also may have been sacred to some pagan water deity, whose powers and attractions would be extinguished by the rites of the new Christian temple. Another factor which may have influenced him was that a hillside was drier and easier to clear of scrub. The summit above the church provided a good look out and until 1839 a lane known as Twattle Alley ran along the southern edge of the churchyard. The name was derived from the old English word tote, a look out, and provided a direct link with Saxon Frome. The monastery was sufficiently close to the network of roads already mentioned to be on the beaten track, but not so near that the contemplative life would be unduly disturbed. It is possible that Aldhelm, continuing his work of conversion in the triangle of land of which Malmesbury formed the apex and Sherborne and Bruton the base, passed this way on his journeys from Bradford-on-Avon, crossing the Frome by the ford close to the present road bridge, at the bottom of North Parade, and continuing on the line of King and Gentle Streets to join the Old Way to Bruton.

Of the Saxon Church and the monastic life which went on within its walls we know little. The two Saxon stones which remain are certainly monumental and no work earlier than about 1160 survives. A question is, however, posed by the unusual position of the tower at St John's, the base of which forms a south transept, and by the exceptionally high, narrow shape of St Andrew's Chapel, which lies behind it to the east. This chapel is early 15th century work, largely renewed by the Victorians, while the base of the tower appears to be of about 1300. The plan may, however, reflect the tower and porticus, or lateral chapel, of the Saxon church. However, there are one or two straws in the wind. Rev W.J. E. Bennett, who carried out the restoration of St John's between 1852 and 1866, was not an archaeologist and had little respect for history. No proper record was made of the old church before it was totally rebuilt. He does, however, tell us in his book, The *Old Church of St John of Froome*, that during the restoration the foundations of the Saxon arcades were discovered west of the porches. If so, and one wonders who judged the foundations to be Saxon, the original church stood between the west front and the middle of the nave. Bennett also says that many Saxon stones were discovered and preserved in the walls of the. tower. Only two of these can now be identified. Prebendary W. E. Daniel, who loomed large as a local historian around 1900, told a meeting of the Somerset Archaeological Society at Frome in 1911 that during this restoration 'the workmen came across certain indications of an early burial which had the indications of a Saxon interment' but that Bennett fearing some antiquary would interfere, had them covered with quicklime. At an earlier meeting of the Society in 1850 it was stated that 'when the wall of the Lady Chapel was being perforated in 1796, the carved head of a dog was found, and on the nostrils of the animal the date 796'. As Arabic numerals did not come into general use in England until towards the end of the Middle Ages, this seems a tall story. It will be noted that there were exactly a thousand years between the date and the find.

The sole authentic remains of the Saxon church to survive are the two sculptured stones built into the wall of the tower. They are believed to be part of a cross, probably fragments of the shaft. This is connected by Bishop Browne, in his life of the saint, with the last journey of St Aldhelm. On the death of Bishop Haeddi of the West Saxons in 703, his diocese, which had been centred on Winchester, was divided into two. The new Bishopric of Sherborne was given to Aldhelm. This was known locally as Selwoodshire, sufficient indication of its heart. Although in his middle sixties—extreme old age by the standards of the day—the saint carried out his episcopal duties with unwearied diligence. During one of his journeys through Selwood, where he had so long laboured in God's vineyard, death overtook him. Aldhelm was near Doulting on the western border of the forest. Nearby 'was a timber church to which at his last breath he ordered himself to be carried as the inhabitants from preceding generations by tradition to this date assert', as William of Malmesbury evidently found out for himself. Today the splendid church of St Aldhelm marks the spot where he died on 25 May, 709.

The saint's body was carried to Malmesbury for burial. The bearers appear to have made seven miles a day and by order of Ecguin, Bishop of Worcester, crosses were erected at each place where his body rested. Frome would seem the obvious stopping place on the first night and it is pleasant to think that our sculptured stones may be part of those crosses 'where many persons afflicted with stubborn distempers, by their earnest prayers were restored to health'. While this cannot be proved, the pieces of Saxon cross found at Frome, Nunney and neighbouring places reveal how firmly Aldhelm planted the power of the cross in Selwood.

Frome prospered exceedingly in the reflected glory of St Aldhelm. In the later Saxon period the town was a place of some importance. It became a royal manor at an early date and escaped assessment for Danegeld, the tax levied to buy off Scandinavian raiders. The Saxon kings had a palace in Frome and hunted in the Forest of Selwood, where a park was already in existence in 1182. King Athelstan held a witenagemot, or great council, at Frome in December 934. This was attended by Wolfstan, Archbishop of York, Wulfhelm, Archbishop of Canterbury, 13 bishops and numerous princes, earls and thegns. Frome also saw a royal death bed, young King Edred dying here on St Clement's Day (23 November), 955. He was buried at Winchester. Edred is described by his contemporary, Bridferth of Romsey, as being constantly oppressed by sickness and of so weak a digestion that he was unable to swallow more than the juices of the food he chewed. This, for some reason, greatly annoyed his guests. The members of his court are said to have deserted his body before it was cold.

It is probable that Frome was a borough in Saxon times for it had a flourishing market and paid the third penny (a tax comprising a third of the profits of the shire court) to the Crown. It may have had a mint, for coins are extant bearing the letters FRO, perhaps an abbreviation for Frome. However, no burgesses are mentioned in the Domesday Book of 1086 and one cannot resist the impression that Frome was in decline by the time of the Norman Conquest. This perhaps connects with William of Malmesbury's suggestion, made in 1125, only a hundred years or so after the last Danish invasion, that St Aldhelm's monastery had been dispersed by the Danes. He tells us the church still stood, but the monastery had gone. In a missionary situation, as at Frome, church and monastery are likely to have been housed together and we are specifically told that the monastery was near the River Frome.

LEFT: Frome grew up in the shadow of St John's: 1 Merchant's Barton, now demolished. RIGHT: St John's in 1866 showing the spring, a decisive factor in the founding of Frome, in its new setting provided by Vicar Bennett. (GHB) BELOW: Of Saxon origin: Frome Market Place, an elegant scene c1850.

ABOVE LEFT: Linking church and market place: King Street about 1850 from a painting by W. W. Wheatley. (JWL) ABOVE RIGHT Another ancient street: Cheap Street at the end of the 19th century. (FM) BOTTOM RIGHT: On the line of a prehistoric trackway: Christchurch Street East, long known as Behind Town, showing the top of Gentle Street as it was in 1863. From a painting by W. W. Wheatley. (SA) BELOW: Two views of Gorehedge, LEFT: a photograph of about 1900 showing a Blue School boy in characteristic uniform, and right 'Bossie' Cray, a butcher and well-known personality (FM) and CENTRE RIGHT : a painting by W. W. Wheatley in 1855. (SA)

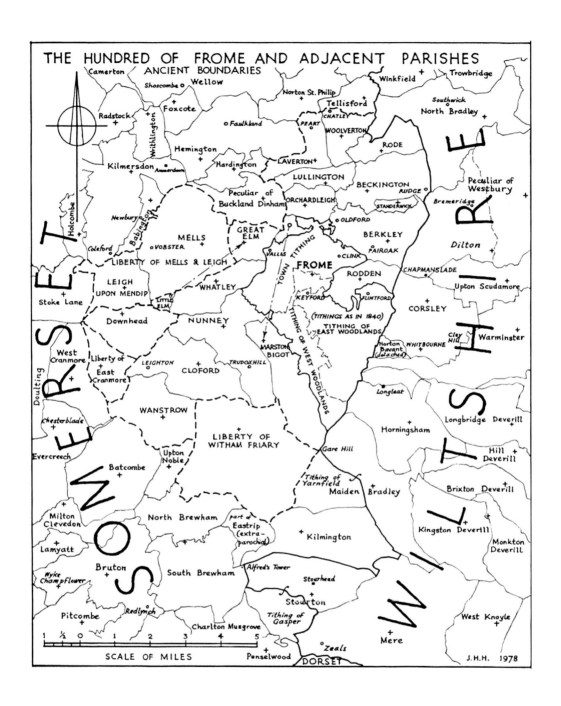

THE HUNDRED OF FROME AND ADJACENT PARISHES
ANCIENT BOUNDARIES

SCALE OF MILES

J.H.H. 1978

26

The Norman Ascendancy

In 1066 Harold II fell at Hastings and William, Duke of Normandy became King of the English. The transfer of power from Saxon thegn to Norman knight was not an overnight occurrence. In some areas, for a period of years the Saxon nobility retained its authority as the Earls Edwin and Morcar did in the North. Frome, being Ancient Demesne of the Crown, became a royal manor and its administration, such as it was, may have continued with a minimum of change. There was also no change of priest at Frome which, the church being a considerable landowner, was a significant factor. The Normans also retained what has been called 'the first fundamental form of English government', the Hundred, a folc gemot, or public assembly, a judicial and administrative body which met in the presence of the King's reeve in Saxon times and later in that of the Sheriff. The system was based on 100 families of freemen each supported by a hide of land, an indeterminate quantity which may have been about 120 acres.

The Hundred as an organ of local government and justice was already old when King Alfred gave it territorial form by dividing the Kingdom of Wessex into shires and the shires into hundreds. Somerset has 40 hundreds of which the Hundred of Frome was originally one of the largest, so big in fact that in the 11th century the Hundreds of Wellow and Kilmersdon were split off from it and the rump further reduced by the creation of the Liberties of Witham Friary (for monks of the enclosed Carthusian Order by Henry II in 1182) and of Mells and Leigh-on-Mendip (granted to the Abbot of Glastonbury in 1281 by Edward I). As we have seen, the Frome Hundred met at Big Tree on Buckland Down, a strangely border position in terms of the reduced area but perfectly central to the original Saxon hundred. Until well into the 18th century the place was known as Modbury (so recorded in 1234), derived from an Old English word meaning a place where moots or assemblies were held and underlining the antiquity of this seat of justice. 'Modbury' was later corrupted to Madborough or Madbarow. Apart from occasional references to meetings of the Hundred Court at 'Modburi' during the Middle Ages there is little recorded about it until a survey was taken of the Hundreds of England during the Commonwealth period about 1650. However, the details given at this date probably reflect traditional procedure. We are told that the Hundreds of Frome and Kilmersdon were within 'the Turn (or jurisdiction) of Modburrgh' in the Hundred of Frome. Frome itself, Cloford, Leighton, Marston Bigot, Wanstrow, Elm, Orchardleigh, Rode, Beckington, Laverton, Standerwick, Lullington and Rodden came within its authority. 'The Sheriff turne courts for Hundreds of Frome and Kilmersdon are kept at a place called Buckland downe alias Modburrgh downe within the months of Easter and Michaelmas according to the custom and usage thereof. The tythingmen (usually the village constable and representative) are to appear at the said courts, and to bring with them a certain number of able and fit persons out of every tything to serve as Jurymen at the said courts which persons are called posts...' These courts were supposed to deal with all public nuisances in the two Hundreds but had been 'much discontinued for divers years past'. The tythingmen and the 'posts' appear to have preferred to stay away, paying their fines of two pence and a penny respectively rather than labour up to Modbury.

According to John Strachey, the Sheriffs tourn was still being held there in the 1730s which, he says, 'shows it a place of remark'.

Buckland Down today is merely a high point to which the essence of history still clings. To Frome people in the 11th century it was a place of retribution where central government, still in its infancy, made a doubtless unwelcome manifestation. King William's clerks, however, were beginning to spin that endless web of bureaucracy which neither they nor the subjects of the Crown in future generations were ever to escape: they set about compiling what has been called our first public record, Domesday Book.

The original parochial area of Frome, thanks to the efforts of St Aldhelm, extended over a wide area. Associated chapels are mentioned in the grant by King Henry I, of Frome Church and its lands to Cirencester Abbey. It is likely that these were the now vanished churches of Egforton (near Fairoak Farm in Berkley parish) and Standerwick. In 1140, Frome Church gave its permission for divine service to be celebrated in the chapel at Egforton three days a week and on saints' days, and a few years later Standerwick Church was granted for life to one Simon, a kinsman of the Lord of the Manor. As late as 1556, the Lords of Woolverton and Rode were making a money payment to Frome for having their burial there, indicating that Frome originally had the parochial rights and was being compensated for the loss of lucrative funeral fees. When in the early 14th century one of the St Maurs of Rode got himself a son and heir, he sent for the priest of Frome to be its godfather. Nevertheless, for all practical purposes it looks as if, by the time of Domesday Book, the parish of St John the Baptist at Frome had already acquired those boundaries which it was to retain basically until after 1840. It was shaped like a somewhat battered and indented lozenge, except on the east where Rodden, itself a Domesday Manor, plunged into its very heart, surrounded on three sides by Frome. Frome parish stretched from Orchardleigh in the north, a manor already in existence in 1086, to come down to an apex below Gare Hill in the south. On the east it was contained by the Wiltshire border and on the west by the ancient manors of Marston, Nunney, Whatley and Elm. It did not, however, contain Spring Gardens, which had an old manorial connection with Marston Bigot and was not transferred to Frome parish until 1885. At the first census in 1801 it was calculated that the parish contained 7,092 acres. Despite adjustments, the present civil parishes of Frome and Selwood adhere broadly to these historic boundaries.

Within this large parish were several jurisdictions. The most important was the royal manor, comprising 50 ploughlands. St John's is one of the few churches to be mentioned in Domesday Book by name. It held eight ploughlands, which it had already possessed in the time of Edward the Confessor, the broad acres, we may surmise, with which St Aldhelm had endowed his monastery, and still retained largely thanks to the successful establishment of Church Right, or the church's perpetual title to the land given to an individual cleric, of which the saint had been a leading exponent. Its wealth reflects the prestige of the founder. In addition there was the Manor of Keyford. This was a Saxon settlement called in Domesday Book Caivel, or Chaivert, and indicating not that it was on a ford, but near a wood where 'keys', probably in the form of pegs or wedges, were made. In the time of Edward the Confessor, the whole of Keyford had belonged to a Saxon called Levedai, but it was now divided between the great Bishop of Coutances and Turstin FitzRolf, who granted their halves to retainers, Nigel and Norman respectively. The division gave rise to Great and Little Keyford, names recorded as early as 1405. For all practical purposes Keyford was later absorbed into the main Manor of Frome, although part passed into the Honour of Gloucester. Keyford in 1086 comprised 1 1/2 ploughlands.

According to Domesday Book the whole parish contained 59 1/2 ploughlands. A ploughland is the equivalent of a hide. Evidently, much land was under cultivation in Frome and there had been substantial clearing of the forest since Aldhelm's days. There were 75 acres of valuable meadow (30 of these belonged to the Church) and 59 acres of pasture. The arable appears to have been grouped in the usual open field system. Later documents mention The Field of Frome, Keyford Field, and North, East and West Fields. The fields were divided into strips which were owned by individuals but, inevitably, farmed in common. Although often called the three field system, there was no sanctity about this number as the unit of rotation was the furlong (made up of a number of strips) which survives as a common field name. Until after the Second World War the ridge and furrow pattern which the open field system imposed on the English landscape was a familiar sight. A few years ago it could be clearly seen at The Mount, Keyford. Modern intensive farming methods have largely swept the evidence away.

The Domesday commissioners list 109 people in the parish of Frome. These would be heads of houses and, however inaccurate, the figure implies a population of 400 or 500. Of the 109, 39 were villeins, tenant farmers of their various lords, having perhaps 30 acres in the common fields and grazing rights, varying in status, but owing labour services to their lord. The villeins were the backbone of the community. Beneath them were the cottars and borders, interchangeable terms for the craftsmen, shepherds and labourers who also held a few acres in return for manorial services. There were 64 of these. Finally, there were six coliberts, freed slaves, who may have worked on the royal demesne. It may be that the villeins represent the village community as opposed to the cottars and borders, but no hard line can be drawn. The rural impression given by the terse details of Domesday Book is overwhelming.

Animals are only recorded on the demesnes, or home farms of the lords of the various manors, but it is clear from the particulars given that Frome followed the rest of the country, in having more sheep and pigs in that order than any other animal. Goats are mentioned in Keyford. Apart from farming, an absolute necessity at a time when a rural community had to be self-sufficient, the sole vaguely industrial activity mentioned is milling. These were grist mills to grind corn. The King had three, which were apparently in good heart, for they paid the handsome sum of 25s to the Crown. There was another mill at Keyford and the church had its own. The market, where local produce could be sold and exchanged with pedlars and chapmen, also flourished, paying the King 46s 8d at a time when a man could live on a few shillings a year.

The total impression of Frome to be gleaned from Domesday is of a village, considerable by the standards of the day, which had gone down in the world since it had been an occasional residence of the Kings of Wessex, yet still a notable place of business. The chief building would have been Aldhelm's stone church in a dominating position on the hillside. The main settlement is likely to have been between St John's and the river and market place without any development on the slope above the church, over which wound the track to the quite independent village of Keyford. The Anglo-Saxon place-names of the parish suggest hamlets scattered through its rural immensity and clustered more thickly near the town itself. Close to Frome were Egford ('the island ford'), first mentioned in the late 13th century and not to be confused with the quite separate parish of Egforton in Berkley, Oldfield (now Spring Gardens), recorded as Aldefeld in 1230, and Clink (Klenec in 1314), so called not from the great prison of that name in Southwark but from clench, Anglo-Saxon for hill.

There seems to have been no woodland worth recording in Keyford, but beyond was an enormous area of trees known in the 13th century as the wood of Selwode and by 1342 as Wodeland, eventually giving its name to two of the three tithings of Frome. This is doubtless synonymous with the wood a league in length and breadth, recorded as being in the royal manor by Domesday. Here at the extremity of the parish under Gare Hill was Langley, the long clearing in the wood, which existed before 1135, while on the western side of the parish next to Marston was Tytherington, another apparently Saxon settlement of uncertain derivation, but perhaps the settlement of Tidhere's people. Some of these places may only have housed a handful of people. Rodden (roe deer valley), although not in the parish of Frome, geographically very much part of it, had only one family living in it in 1255 and three householders were mentioned there in the lay subsidy list of 1327. It has been suggested that there was another settlement at Pikewell opposite Spring Gardens under Orchardleigh Down,to whose church some institutions of clergy are recorded in the 14th century. However, it is likely that this is an alternative name for Berkley, which contained an area called Pikwell or Pickwells, and for whose church no institutions are recorded before 1406. It is notable that the first recorded incumbent of Pikewell was appointed by the Lord of Berkley. Domesday says nothing of the Royal Forest of Selwood subject to its own laws above and outside those of the Realm, and defended by rapacious foresters responsible only to the King himself, but its existence affected the people of Frome nearly and badly. Until an attempt was made to push back its frontiers in 1219, the foresters claimed Keyford, Rodden, Feltham and Flintford as within the bounds, extending their authority to the gates of Frome itself.

The bald statement in Domesday Book that 'Reinbald is priest there' conceals rather than reveals the identity of the most important politician ever to be connected with Frome. Reinbald was, in fact, a favourite of King Edward the Confessor and probably came over with him to England when the king was summoned from his Norman exile to succeed the Danish Hardicanute in 1042. His name suggests that he was of Frankish origin. Reinbald was one of the royal clerks, involved in most aspects of government,and may have served as Chancellor. He amassed vast estates and held 'sixteen churches, rich in tithe and glebe'. Horace Round has called him the first great pluralist, or holder of multiple church benefices. Among other offices, he was Dean of the College of Prebendaries at Cirencester, and his name is found on most of the great charters of the reign.

Reinbald was granted exceptional privileges, as when King Edward informed 'the bishops, earls, sheriffs, and thegns in the shires where Reinbald his priest has land and men, that he is to have rights over his land and men as fully as any of his predecessors.. .and that his writ shall be as much as a diocesan bishop'. William I found his experience and official knowledge useful, so Reinbald survived the change of dynasty at Senlac in 1066. Indeed, he received a remarkable favour from the new king,being granted all his land as fully and completely as he held it under King Edward, the monarch adding with an eye to the troubled times 'I will not that any (if he value my friendship) shall deprive him of aught I have given him'.

We do not know the date when this wily trimmer died. He was already old in 1086; he perhaps survived into the reign of Henry I. Leland saw his tomb in Cirencester Abbey, a cross of white marble inscribed: Hic Jacet Rembaldus, presbyter, quondam huius ecclesiae Decanus et tempore Edwardi Regis Angliae Cancellarius. (Here lies Reinbald the priest, former Dean of this Church and Chancellor of England in the time of King Edward).

Rodden: the old home of the A'Court family by W.W. Wheatley, 1844. (SA)

LEFT: The road to Modbury: Buckland Dinham c1860. (AD) RIGHT: Traditionally said to occupy the site of the Manor House of Egford: Maed House, later home of Mrs Elizabeth Rowe. (CB) BELOW: Once part of the parish of Frome: Rode Church and ancient ritual dance by W.W. Wheatley. (SA)

ABOVE: In 1086 Frome Market paid yearly dues of 46s 8d to the Crown: one of the earliest photographs taken before 1871. BELOW: Remains of the mediaeval strip system at the Mount, Keyford, c1960. (FM)

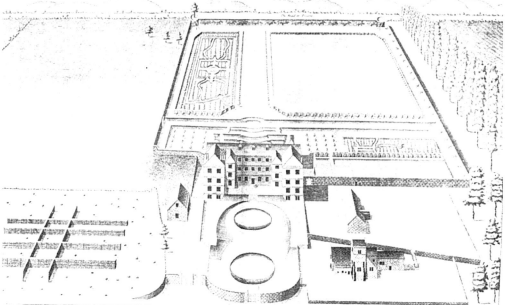

ABOVE: The old Manor House of Orchardleigh, taken down in 1860. (AD) BELOW: Marston Bigot was a Norman manor and Marston House, seen here as it was in 1739, the future home of the Lords of the Manor of Frome (SRO)

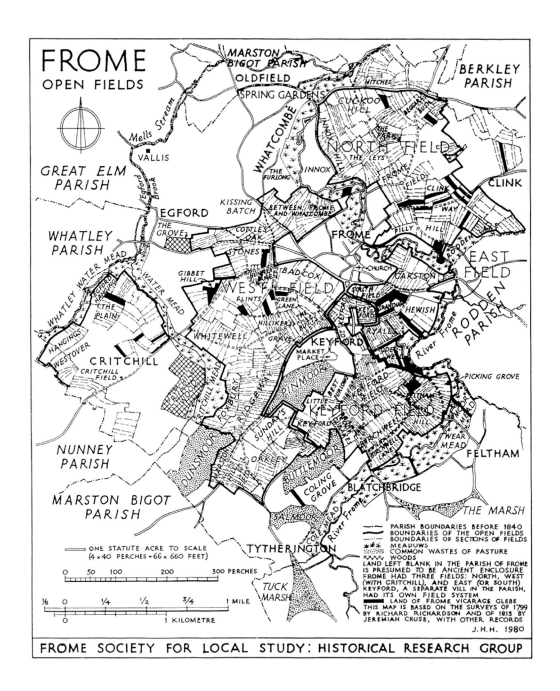

FROME
OPEN FIELDS

MARSTON BIGOT PARISH
OLDFIELD
SPRING GARDENS
BERKLEY PARISH

Mells Stream
VALLIS

GREAT ELM PARISH

Egford Brook

KISSING BATCH

WHATCOMBE
THE FURLONG
INNOX

CUCKOO HILL
THE PARK
THE LEYS
NORTH FIELD
HITCHES

FROME
FIELD
CLINK WAY
CLINK

EGFORD
THE GROVE

WHATLEY PARISH

COTTLE'S OAK
STONES

BETWEEN FROME AND WHATCOMBE

FROME

PILLY HILL

CHURCH
MARSTON
EAST FIELD

WHATLEY WATER MEAD
EGFORD HANGING
THE PLAIN

WATER MEAD

GIBBET HILL

BADCOX

WEST FIELD
FLINTS
GREEN LANE
HILLIKERS
THE BUTTS

SOUTH FIELD
KEYFORD
GRANDHAM
HEWISH
RYALLS

RODDEN PARISH

River Frome

HANGINGS
WESTOVER

CRITCHILL
CRITCHILL FIELD

WHITEWELL

GRAVE

KEYFORD
MARKET PLACE

PICKING GROVE

DINMOOR

LITTLE KEYFORD

KEYFORD FIELD
FEATHAM'S HILL

WEAR MEAD
FELTHAM

NUNNEY PARISH

SUNDAYS HILL

OAKLEY

BRINCHWELL

BUTLEMOOR

COLING GROVE

BLATCHBRIDGE

THE MARSH

MARSTON BIGOT PARISH

SALMOOR

COLE MEAD
River Frome

TYTHERINGTON

TUCK MARSH

PARISH BOUNDARIES BEFORE 1840
BOUNDARIES OF THE OPEN FIELDS
BOUNDARIES OF SECTIONS OF FIELDS
MEADOWS
COMMON WASTES OF PASTURE
WOODS
LAND LEFT BLANK IN THE PARISH OF FROME
IS PRESUMED TO BE ANCIENT ENCLOSURE
FROME HAD THREE FIELDS: NORTH, WEST
(WITH CRITCHILL), AND EAST (OR SOUTH)
KEYFORD, A SEPARATE VILL IN THE PARISH,
HAD ITS OWN FIELD SYSTEM
LAND OF FROME VICARAGE GLEBE
THIS MAP IS BASED ON THE SURVEYS OF 1799
BY RICHARD RICHARDSON AND OF 1813 BY
JEREMIAH CRUSE, WITH OTHER RECORDS
J.H.H. 1980

ONE STATUTE ACRE TO SCALE
(4 x 40 PERCHES = 66 x 660 FEET)

0   50   100   200   300 PERCHES

1/8   0   1/4   1/2   3/4   1 MILE

0   1 KILOMETRE

FROME SOCIETY FOR LOCAL STUDY: HISTORICAL RESEARCH GROUP

Abbot and Lord

It is unlikely that so great a man as Reinbald was often at Frome and no doubt the parish was served by curates. But Reinbald's connection with Cirencester ensured that Frome and that pleasant Gloucestershire town should be linked for more than 400 years. On Reinbald's death, his great estates passed to the Crown. In 1133, Henry I founded Cirencester Abbey, which foundation took the place of the college with which Reinbald had been connected. In a fine and appropriate gesture, Henry endowed the new abbey with the 'whole property of Reinbald the priest, both in lands and church'. These included: 'In Froome, the church with its lands, chapels, and tithes, and all other things, as well in the plain as in the forest, pertaining to the said church'. This property can be largely equated with the later tithing of West Woodlands but including a farm in East Woodlands already called La Bolwe in 1270, and long known as Abbot's Bollow. The main estate was in two sections: a block of property close to the town and another substantial holding in the hinterland. The boundaries of the first stretched from Wallbridge to Vicarage Street along Eagle Lane to touch the Market Place (this was before the cutting of Bath Street), before proceeding by way of Stony Street and Sheppards Barton to Christchurch Street West, and coming back to Wallbridge via Broadway, Keyford Elm and Adderwell. St John's Church was safely inside these boundaries. A narrow corridor of land linked this estate, which was to become increasingly urban, with the agricultural land and woods which ran down the parish boundary of Marston Bigot on the line of Sunday's Hill (derived from the Somedemede mentioned in a charter of 1343), Tytherington, Tuckmarsh (Tokkemerssh in 1392), Waldyke (in Marston Bigot), Abbot's Moor, and, right at the end against the Wiltshire border, Langley.

The Abbot of Cirencester became landlord of these extensive possessions and also Rector (from the Latin *ruler*) of Frome. From this fact his lands became known as the Rectorial Manor or the Manor of Frome Rectory. As lord he was entitled to labour or military services from his tenants, (as a baron of the Kingdom he had to supply his quota of armed men to the King in time of war) and as rector he had a right to the great tithes. At least since the eighth century each householder had been required to give a tenth of his produce towards the upkeep of the local clergy. As head of a great monastic establishment, the Abbot could not be expected to serve the cure himself, and appointed a vicar (from the latin for deputy) to represent him. Nevertheless, it was customary for the Rector to cream off the great tithes, such as corn, hay and wood, which were fairly easy to collect and leave the small tithes, minor produce and some labour services, for the upkeep of the Vicar.

At Frome a more generous arrangement obtained. The Abbot kept all the tithes great and small but endowed his vicar with a small estate which became known as the Manor of Frome Vicarage. This institution, which was quite separate from the glebe or church lands, lasted into the 20th century and consisted of the Vicarage, the cottage adjoining it to the east, a number of cottages on the south side of Vicarage Street (Nos 23 to 29) and the Auction Mart, the marble works in Portway with the former Great Western Hotel adjoining it to the east, and a range of buildings in Palmer Street where Cockey's iron foundry stood. This endowment had already been made by the middle of the 13th century when a charter of Roger Medicus

(Roger the doctor) granting land in Frome to the Abbot, mentions half an acre ' at the head of the land of the Vicar of Frome along the road to Walebrigge'. Up to 1244, the vicar appears to have had some right to tithe as well, but in that year gave it up in return for a pension of 20s. He in turn rendered an ancient pension of 40s to the Abbot, perhaps in return for his manor. This was a substantial sum, perhaps £4,000 in today's money.

The Abbot, too, had a house at Frome—his Rectory—although he was rarely there himself, and in later years it was let out. It stood high above the vicarage on the site of St John's Infant School in Christchurch Street East, with a great cruciform tithe barn beside it, which survived well into the 19th century. The abbots were sticklers for their dues in this respect and in 1230 two local farmers, Arnold of Frome and Robert le Noreis, were forced to acknowledge that they were bound to pay him their tithes of corn before paying their labourers. No 27, Vicarage Street, notable for its wide, hood-moulded archway, is associated in Frome tradition with the residence of the abbot's bailiff. It is directly below the Rectory site and dates from about 1525, just within the monastic period. By this date, the abbots were letting their property on long lease and farming out the tithes in return for a fixed payment, and as the house was part of the Vicarage Manor anyway, the story lacks substance. The archway does not fit and may well have been brought from elsewhere. However, some such arrangement is confirmed by an entry in the 1392 Cirencester Abbey rental, by which Matthew Craas had a garden in Vicarage Street with a way out of the Lord's Barton, or yard. From the middle of the 13th century, the Rectory was known as the Abbot's Court because the Manorial Court, which dealt with petty offences, local administration and disputes between lord and tenant, met there, presided over by the Abbot's *prepositus*, steward or reeve, an important man in Frome and a leading townsman. Just before the dissolution of Cirencester Abbey in 1538 the Rectory was let to Alice West and described as the 'scyte of the Manor or parsonage, one house, a barne, a stable, a dovehouse all covered with tyle, a garden an orchard and a backside containing by estimation 2 acres, a close of pasture over against the ferme gate'. The home farm consisted of Bollow, various closes of pasture called Crosses, Shawe, Spurmead, Colyn grove and Horsechurchhay, 37 acres of arable land lying together in furlongs 'on the west part of Frome', 13 acres of arable called Okeleyes, a tithe barn with a pasture called Papps at Berkley, Cabell's Barn, and a cottage 'adjoining to the great barn'.

Although influential in Frome, the Abbot of Cirencester did not have matters all his own way. Early in the 12th century Henry I gave the royal Manor of Frome, together with the Lordship of the Hundred, to one of the greatest of his barons, Roger de Courcelles. Roger, who held 108 Manors *in capite*, that is as a tenant-in-chief direct from the Crown, as well as others from Glastonbury Abbey, already had some property near the town including Witham, Standerwick, and Egforton, but Frome was the plum. Roger probably died before 1135 (we last hear of him in 1121) and his great inheritance was broken up under mysterious circumstances, much of his property passing to the Malet family. However, his son Wandrille salvaged something from the wreck and in 1161 held ten knight's fees in Somerset. A knight's fee is exactly that: the amount of land needed to maintain a knight and his family for a year. It varied considerably according to the quality of the soil. The Manor of Frome which Wandrille managed to retain out of his father's vast estates, was optimistically considered to make a single knight's fee, but later found to be worth only half. Despite this there is some evidence that Wandrille de Courcelles made Frome his chief seat and he may have built the original manor-house at Vallis. Although the name does not appear until 1318, as 'Faleise', it derives direct from a Norman-French word meaning a cliff, which suggests an early origin. The position on the edge of the escarpment, protected on three sides by the cliffs which rise out of the gorge of the Egford Brook, is immensely strong and John Skinner, the Camerton antiquary, purported to see fortifications there on a visit in 1838. It seems unlikely that Wandrille would have wanted to live in the town: Vallis was sufficiently near to keep an eye on it, while better placed for hunting and recreation. All that is known for certain is that he had a house at Frome, presumably remote from the church, for between 1155 and 1166 he was granted a licence to have an oratory in his house because of his 'obvious illness'. Despite this he was still living in 1170. His descendants were to remain Lords of Frome for nearly 600 years.

It was probably Wandrille de Courcelles who rebuilt St Aldhelm's Saxon church which William of Malmesbury had seen still there in 1125. The licence for Wandrille to have an oratory was given not only because of his illness but also because of his benefactions to St John's Church. Judging by the high quality of the remaining work, no expense was spared. The doorway to the Lady Chapel, with its deep bowtell moulding is particularly fine and, as Dr John Harvey has pointed out, related to the style of the first work at Wells Cathedral except, as it is earlier, it is round-headed instead of pointed. The adjoining blind niche and a piscina are part of the same reconstruction and the north and south doors, although renewed, contain some of the old Norman stones. This rebuilding took place about 1160 and left the church a broadly cruciform structure, nave and chancel flanked by a short tower to the south and by the Lady Chapel to the north. The entrance to the Lady Chapel was never an outside doorway, so presumably there was another chapel on the site of the present Baptistry.

Wandrille's benefactions also included the gift of 14 acres of land in 'Colegrava' (presumably Collingrove adjoining Viney Lane) and other property, to the brethren of St Mary of Langley. One of the witnesses to Wandrille's charter is Alfred (Aluredus) the priest, perhaps an early incumbent of Frome, or the great man's chaplain. The foundation of a chapel may have been an attempt to bring the influence of the church to bear on this remote part of the parish, whose thick woods were long the refuge of thieves and desperadoes. Langley had belonged to Frome Church before the time of Henry I, who ejected men from the forest there, presumably outlaws who had occupied it. The King seems then to have omitted to give it back and it was returned to Cirencester Abbey by the Empress Matilda, daughter of Henry I, in 1141. The building of the Chapel may have followed this recovery. However, according to a curious 15th century *inspeximus*, a resume of legal evidence, at Longleat House, Langley was founded by St Algar and endowed with the Manor of Langley, to provide money for the upkeep of three chaplains to pray for his soul or that of King Edward, perhaps Edward the Elder (901-925), son of King Alfred. Algar was Bishop of Crediton from 942 to 953, but the idea of a chantry chapel to pray for the souls of the dead is a much later development not heard of before 1235. The site is now known as St Algar's Farm and is first mentioned by that name in a will of 1361. According to Leland, writing about 1540, here were 'buryed the Bones of St Algar of late tyms superstitiously soute of the folisch Commune People'. Francis Thynne, of the Longleat family, recorded at the end of the 16th century how it was the custom there for pilgrims to 'ringe a little bell with their teeth'. About 1170, the brethren received some land 'which lies beyond the water of Frome' and part of a wood from Richard son of Odo, of Marston, and sixty years later 'the grove which Swonhilda of the Bridge sometime held' from Richard Bigot. By 1235, the brethren appear to have drifted over the border into Wiltshire to found Longleat Priory, changing their dedication from St Mary to St Radagond, but the Langley Chapel continued and became associated with the name of St Algar. It is possible that this remote place is the leper house in Selwode to which Hugh of Wells, Bishop of Lincoln, left money in 1235. There was a leper hospital for women just up the road at Maiden Bradley, but Bishop Hugh clearly meant a male establishment. In this connection it is significant that when John Crede, priest of the Chantry Chapel of St Andrew in Frome Church, became leprous in 1448 he applied to the Bishop to retire to a cell in the precincts of St Algar's Chapel. He survived there four years. At times services were much neglected—about 1420 they were said to have been so for 40 years past—but the Chapel remained and a lease of 1539 describes 'the manor of ffarm of Langley with all houses and buildings thereto appteyninge, viz: a house, a chappell, a stable or oxhouse, all stone tyled, a thatched barn, a garden and orchard'. There was also a close of pasture called Aker Heyes, perhaps indicating the former residence of an anchorite or hermit.

While prepared to rebuild and endow churches to the glory of God and to pay due obeisance to the Abbot of Cirencester in his role as a great prelate, Wandrille de Courcelles resisted his pretensions as feudal baron and rural landowner. Trouble was caused by the dues, described as suits and customs but boiling down in the final resort to hard cash, claimed by Wandrille as Lord of the Hundred from the abbot's tenants in Frome. The abbot resisted these and the dispute simmered for more than 50 years. Matters were so hot around 1164 that Wandrille seized some of the abbatial property in Frome, and Queen Eleanor, acting as regent for Henry II who was in France, had to intervene, forbidding Wandrille to trouble the Abbot and ordering him to restore anything of theirs he had taken,Frome Church being under the special protection of sovereigns. Wandrille no doubt needed the money: he was always in arrears with his taxes, at one time owing 40 marks (a mark was 13s 4d) of which he paid £8 17s 4d on account. There is no record that he ever paid the remaining £17 16s 0d. The dispute with Cirencester was carried on by Wandrille's son, Hugh who lived until 1186 or 1187 and the King again had to intervene, telling Hugh to allow the Canons to enjoy Frome Church peacefully and not to trouble them concerning its rights. Under Hugh's son, Wandrille II de Courcelles, the matter was settled in 1194 by agreement, a final concord as it was pleasantly called, but there was nothing final about it and it was not until 1219 that Wandrille's son-in-law, Ralph FitzBernard, agreed with the Abbot to drop his demands in return for 13 marks, the equivalent today of several thousand pounds. Despite this agreement, the lord's haywards continued to enter two pastures of the abbot called Woodshaw and Ryecroft near Blakebrigg (Blatchbridge) until William Branch agreed to desist about the year 1260.

Wandrille de Courcelles was the last of the senior line, although a junior branch flourished in Frome into the 14th century. He died in or soon after 1212, leaving an only daughter Alianor, or Eleanor, whose marriage was in the gift of the Crown. Her land of Frome was worth £30 so she was a *partie* worth having. Either as a mark of favour or for a price, King John gave her to Ralph FitzBernard who, however, threw in his lot with the barons who were trying to secure Magna Carta. Ralph was in possession before 1 November 1215 when as a result of his transgressions the King ordered 'the Manor of Frome which was of Ralph the son of Bernard, which the Lord King gave to him' to be put into the possession of his natural son, Oliver. This young man, one of the King's many illegitimate children, received lands in Kent in 1213 and died on crusade at Damietta six years later. Ralph made his peace with William Marshall, the regent for the infant Henry III, in 1217, receiving letters of safe conduct in order to do so. It is probable that he recovered the Manor of Frome after Oliver's death. In 1235 Ralph received royal permission to cut 10 oaks 'in his wood of Frome which is within the King's Forest to build himself a lodge at Frome'. The oaks probably came from the wood of Selwode in East Woodlands which, although Ralph's property, came under the Forest Law and were not his to do with as he pleased. However, he was allowed to draw the trees from the wood without paying cheminage, a toll normally extracted to pay for the damage caused by those who used the forest tracks. It is likely that Ralph used the wood to build a new manor house at Vallis. No architectural remains of this date are to be seen at Vallis today, although the distinguished architect Harold Brakespear, who examined the house in 1927, saw a pointed arch leading from the hall to the cross wing, which he believed to be 14th century.

By his wife Alianor, Ralph FitzBernard had an only daughter Joanna who married William Branch. He was a Norfolk baron who possessed land at Gresham and may have been the son of that Peter Branch whose grant of lands at Salthouse and Kelling in Norfolk was confirmed by William's son Nicholas in 1321. Ralph was dead by 1238 when Joanna's custody and marriage were granted to Simon de Esteilland. On. 15 August 1238 Alianor was ordered to deliver her children to the King's messengers, she having been entrusted with them because of their tender years. Simon can have lost no time in arranging Joanna's marriage, no doubt in return for a handsome sum, to William Branch who was established in Frome the same year, when he acted as surety for the Abbot of Cirencester in his dispute with Richard Bigot, of Marston, over common of pasture in Thickthorn Wood. In 1240, he paid 100s for the relief, or entry fee, on being put in possession of his wife's inheritance.

William Branch and his son Nicholas, born about 1251, were high in the favour of that most generous of Kings, Henry III. In 1270, William and Joanna secured from the Crown the grant of a fair to be held every year at Frome for three days on the eve, day and morrow of the Nativity of the Blessed Mary (7-9 September), as well as the right to a market every week on Saturday. The market, presumably a confirmation of one which had long existed by prescription, is with us yet and the fair is still represented by Frome cheese show and carnival. William also received the right of free warren in his demesne lands of Frome and Elm, which meant that he could hunt all the beasts of the chase except the royal deer. Shortly before his death in 1271, William was given permission to take 12 roe buck in the Forest of Selwood but, alas, was by then too infirm to avail himself of the privilege, which was passed on by the King to Nicholas Branch. This young man, described as King's yeoman, was in the personal service of Henry III and the inference can be drawn that the King was especially attracted to him. He was showered with gifts and favours: a tun of wine 'of the gift of the King', 24 rabbits for his warren, six oaks for building from the Forest of Axisholt, a licence to hunt with his own dogs, hare, fox, badger and cat in all the forests of Somerset and Wiltshire. At his instance, as is especially recorded, his younger brother Thomas was pardoned for trespass in the King's forests, and his parents received a grant from the Crown of the Manor of Frome in perpetuity. After his father's death, Nicholas was granted his mother's marriage, more apparently to safeguard her from an unwelcome match than for its potential value. One of William Branch's last acts was to endow his son Thomas with extensive lands in East Woodlands, Egford, and Whatcombe. These later formed the Manor of Frome Egford. Thomas Branch's daughter, Joanna, married Henry de Merlaund, of Orchardleigh, taking these properties with her. William Branch's Charter of Foundation still exists among the muniments at Orchardleigh Park together with Joanna Branch's confirmation, granted 'in lawful widowhood' and bearing in brown wax her seal, inscribed with her name and a falcon leaving a gauntleted hand to pounce on another bird. She died in 1279 leaving, beside the Manor of Frome, a virgate (normally about 30 acres) of land in Elm and two in Rodden.

LEFT: The mediaeval church: two photographs of the north side of St John's showing it and the Lady Chapel before the restoration of 1860-66. (JWL) BELOW: St John's: the east side of the Lady Chapel before the Victorian restoration. (JWL) ABOVE : Entrance to the Lady Chapel at St John's, probably part of the rebuilding of the church, 1160-70. (FM) RIGHT: Occupying the site of the mediaeval vicarage: Frome Vicarage from a drawing by Rev John Skinner, 1821. (FM) RIGHT: Charter, cl260 by which Ralph, son of Ernald of Frome, granted his brother Walter, land in the Field of Frome. (AD) BELOW RIGHT: Charter of Joanna Branch, 1271 to 1279, confirming the grant of the Manor of Frome Egford to her son, Thomas. (AD)

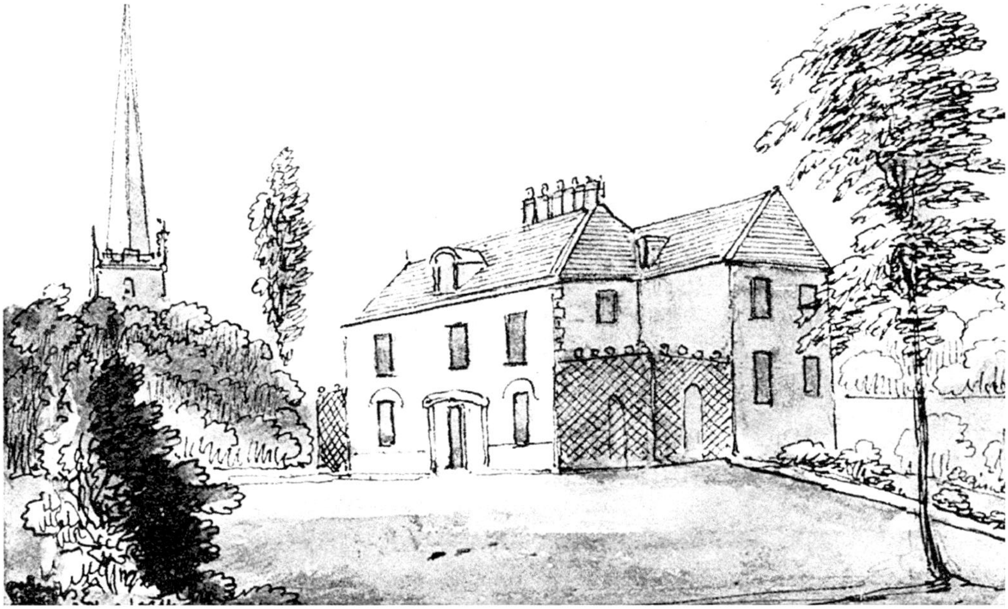

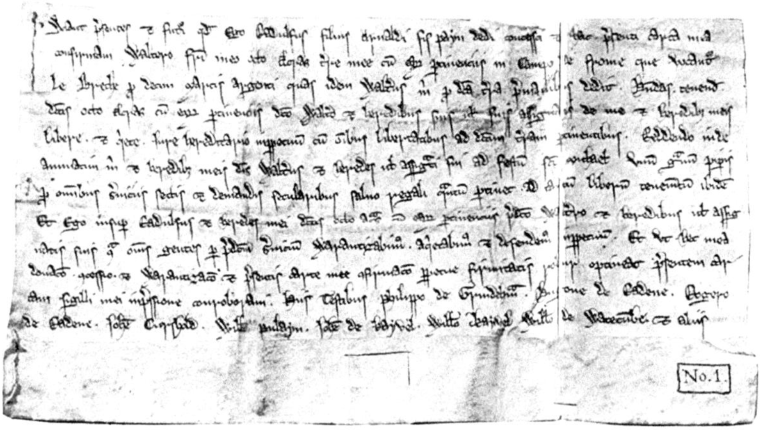
No.1.

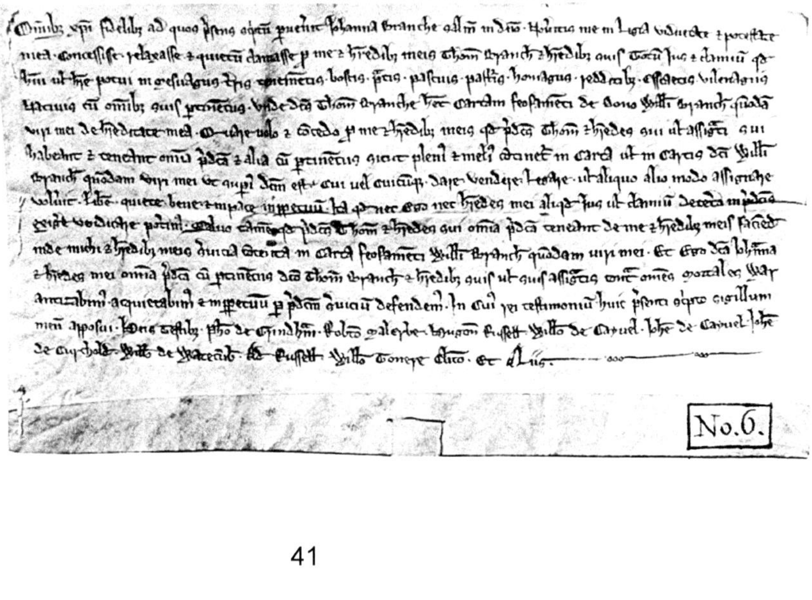
No.6.

ABOVE LEFT: The interior of the Great Hall at Vallis in 1844 from a painting by W.W. Wheatley; (SAS) RIGHT: reduced to a shell cl955; (T) CENTRE RIGHT: in 1974, (CB) and BELOW: the interior, with the roof more or less intact. (FM) CENTRE LEFT: The Manor House at Vallis by W.W. Wheatley, 1844. The Great Hall, which stood on the right, appears to have been deliberately omitted, (SAS) and BELOW: the manor cl860, an unusual view from the west showing the hall and private apartments.

Root and Branch

Frome's proximity to the Royal Forest of Selwood was a mixed blessing. The Forest was subject to a particular body of law which had as its object the preservation of the King's deer. Unfortunately, although the King controlled the forest he did not necessarily own all the land that comprised it. Selwood contained chapels, houses, woods and fields, the interests of whose inhabitants and cultivators came a poor second to the interests and well-being of the deer. St Hugh of Lincoln who was for seven years from 1179 to 1186 Prior of the Carthusian monastery of Witham, which was surrounded by the royal forest, knew the foresters at first hand, detested them and 'felt extreme indignation at the cruel way in which the poor country people were treated by the foresters and forest laws'. Forest did not then have its present meaning of a vast collection of trees; it meant an area beyond the common law of the land and the normal activities of the community, from the latin *foras*, outside. St Hugh, in his indignation, made a pun on the word: 'Forester means a man who remains outside' (*forestarius, foris stare*), he said, 'yes, that is the right name for them, for they will remain outside the Kingdom of God'. In 1277, the men of Somerset complained at an inquisition that too many foresters were appointed and that they were asked to pay for them; that the foresters collected their corn and made ale from it, which they then compelled the inhabitants to buy; that they took their lambs and pigs and cut down their trees for fuel; that they charged them chiminage when it was not due. These exactions were much more resented than the restrictions on hunting or woodcutting. Some took refuge in outlawry, such as those who attacked and robbed the King's clerk, Roger de Evesham and presumably stole the taxes he was taking to London.

The perambulations of 1219, 1279, and 1300 threw back the bounds of the forest as far as they concerned Frome, to the extreme south-eastern corner of the parish, leaving within them Roddenbury and Timber Hills, Longleat Woods (the wood of Selwode), Abbots Moor, and Langley. An instance of the difficulties experienced by holding land within the forest was revealed at the Forest Pleas held at Ilchester in 1270, when the Abbot of Cirencester was summoned to answer for an enclosure of his at Langley. The Abbot had to put up with the deer browsing his good herbage there; the trouble was that, although they could get in fairly easily, they could only get out through one or two breaches in the bank, where poachers awaited them, to the great loss of the forest. The enclosure was seized by the Crown until the Abbot could prove title. When he did so he was promptly fined 10 marks.

The hazardous delights of poaching the King's deer were the other side of the coin. The sport was indulged in by all classes of local people both in Frome and the surrounding villages. Even the Verderer, Henry de Montfort, of Nunney, was not above it and was himself imprisoned at Ilchester for his pains. In 1261, members of the household of Witham Charterhouse entered the forest with bows and arrows, crossbows, hatchets, nets and dogs. They killed a doe which was taken to the Charterhouse. Some were caught. The others, however, were resolute and forcibly rescued their implements from the Verderer at Nunney.

The Forest pleas held at Ilchester in 1257 contain the names of 21 men from the parish of Frome caught poaching and fined, usually 12d each. They included Arnold and Adam Tyrel, John and Hugh Pylie, Richard de Hyreberne and Ralph de Cleybrugge. The men of

Tytherington and Waldyke, being closer to the forest, had greater opportunities. Six of those caught came from Tytherington, among them Robert Faber ('smith) and John le Conare, evidently the keeper of a rabbit warren. Geoffrey Athelem of 'Waldich' had died since his offence. Although the actual area of the forest was much reduced since the 12th century, the provisions of the Forest Law were to remain a thorn in the side of those who owned land within its purlieus, until the disafforestation in 1630. The King himself had a hunting seat at Brewham Lodge within ten miles of Frome, referred to in 1298 as 'the hall of the Lord King' (*portam aule domini regis*) and still containing a pretty lodge, tiled and moated, as late as 1550. Another local celebrity was Richard, Earl of Cornwall, brother of Henry III, who had been elected Holy Roman Emperor and was known as the King of the Romans. He owned until his death in 1271, when it was given to Witham Priory, the Manor of Monksham in Marston, whence his tenants plagued the Abbot of Cirencester, by making encroachments on his land at Waldyke.

King Edward I visited Frome on Holy Rood Day (14 September) 1276 on his way to Keynsham, but no details are mentioned. He would have found a small but busy town still largely grouped between the church and the River. The two earliest street names recorded in charters of about 1300 are Church Slope and Hunger Lane. Hunger Lane (from Old English *hangra*, land on a steep slope) is the old name for Gentle Street. Two houses on the west part of the church are mentioned in a charter of 1215, and by 1300 there were many houses round the churchyard and on Church Slope, referred to in an early 14th century charter as *Scaleram Cimiterii*. Houses were built and enlarged and the future Gentle Street developed. In 1300, William Page sold to the Abbot of Cirencester a building plot 'in the street called Hunger Lane' which appears to have been on the site of Argyll House and Oriel Lodge. A few years earlier Ralph, son of Ernald of Frome, sold a house with an enclosed garden opposite the house of John Ascel on *magno vico* (the main street) of Frome. It is likely that there was some development in Vicarage Street although it does not appear by name until 1392 (Vicarestret). Cheap Street must also have existed although it is not mentioned until 1500. 'Brodeweye' (Broadway) is mentioned in a charter dating from shortly before 1271. Both Cotele's Oak, then known as Cotele's Ash (Cotelisasse or *Fraxinum Cotelli*) and Garston were in the fields. Wallbridge (Walebrige) and Clink, where Clenkhege was a well known boundary mark, were quite separate from the town.

It is probable that the town advanced up the slopes of Catherine Hill after the foundation of the free Chapel of St Katherine. Nothing is known of its origins but as the patronage was in the hands of Richard de Wynslade, son-in-law of Nicholas Branch in 1326, it looks as if it was founded by the Branch family. No royal licence is recorded, which indicates that the chapel may have come into existence before the Statute of Mortmain in 1279 tightened up on grants of land to the church. It first appears in about 1300 when Hugh, Chaplain of St Katerene witnessed a local charter. In 1327 he was fined 4d by the Manorial Court of Egford for allowing four of his oxen to stray into a field called Bataylmed. Before 1380, its original endowment was augmented by a gift of property from Lawrence Walsh, its chaplain. The lands, which stretched from the banks of the Frome, over the modern Cork Street (formerly Hill Lane) and up the hill into the Trinity area came to be known as the Manor of St Katherine, and were to play an important part in the future development of Frome. The exact site of the chapel is uncertain. Because the 1774 map of Frome marks a 'supposed old nunnery' at what is now Catherine Hill, the shop and house on the left going up Sheppard Barton Steps, this has always been held to be the site of St Katherine's Chapel. That it retains the vestiges of a mediaeval house, where, in 1929, Dom Ethelbert Horne, of Downside Abbey, found the remains of a large moulded doorway which he pronounced to be of the late 14th century, and a 'church window', has helped. However, John Strachey records a still earlier tradition—he was active between 1725 and 1740—that 'ye site of ye Chantry of St Catherine... is probably the house of Mr Bull'.

In his *History of Somerset*, published in 1791, Rev John Collinson repeats this information, adding that 'in part of the town called Hill Lane, once stood an old building, by tradition a priory, of which there now remains but a small part which is converted into a cellar within a house built by Mr. Bull'. Hall House, the home of the Bulls, one of Frome's clothier families, has now gone the way of the world and is covered by Westway, but it stood on Chantry land and was much closer to the mansion house of its priests (which the researches of Derek Gill have shown to have been where the Old Presbytery above Cork Street now stands), than a building on the top of Catherine Hill. Moreover, in 1476, St Katherine's Chapel is said to be in the west end of Frome, a term which in recent times has meant the area behind Messrs Singers' factory. Catherine Hill and Palmer Street, long known as Katherine Street, like Catherine Stile and Great Katherine Street in the Trinity area, acquired their names not because they led to the chapel, but because it owned property in them. According to a conveyance of 1534 when Robert Leversedge sold the advowson, as the right of presenting the priest to the living was called, to Sir Walter Hungerford, there was a fair and market held near St Katherine's Chapel. It would certainly have been more convenient to hold this in the field adjoining the Cork Street site, long known as Bull's Meadow, than on Catherine Hill. In the 19th century, this fair was still held in Cross Street, as the central part of Trinity Street was known, and a right of toll over anyone coming up Whittox Lane was exercised by the King's Arms Inn. The fair was discontinued when the Frome Market Company was set up in 1875.

St John's Church was not neglected. There was a substantial rebuilding of the Norman Church between 1280 and 1300, including the tower (to a line below the present belfry) which may have been completed by a wooden spire, chancel, and three eastern bays of the nave. All this, except for the western face of the tower, was much renewed by the Victorians. Some 50 years later the Lady Chapel was extended northwards, the two periods of work being defined by the different levels of string course (a projecting band of stone running horizontally) on the eastern outside wall. The Lady Chapel, although endowed as a chantry by several Frome families, was the property of the Lord of the Manor and the burial place of successive holders of this rank and position until 1856. By 1314, this manor was becoming known as that of Frome Branch, or, after the residence of its Lords, Frome-Vallis, to distinguish it from other holdings in the parish.

Nicholas Branch presided over a closely knit society of local landowners and rich merchants judging by the number of local charters which survive, where they acted as witnesses in each other's legal transactions. It is unlikely that they all gathered together when some obscure parcel of land was granted to another. Perhaps they had some standing arrangement, whereby their names were appended to documents. Nevertheless, men like William Portbref, of Flintford, John de Courcelles, Gilbert Michel, of Feltham, William Polayn, of Keyford, Henry de Merlaund, of Orchardleigh, Nicholas de la Mare and Geoffrey de Montfort, of Nunney, Philip de Grindeham (Grandon in East Woodlands), John de Flory, of Cloford, met not only about land transactions, but also about the administration of justice, and for recreation. When Nicholas Branch's son, Andrew was born in 1312 Robert Redespray rode from Frome to announce the birth to the local notables who were feasting (in *convivio*) with John de Dinham in his hall at Buckland. When in 1314 Thomas Southover married Robergia de Merlaund, the respective parents no doubt came together for some hard bargaining before Henry de Merlaund agreed to give the happy pair the 29s 8d rent he had heretofore received from the parents, the rights he had in a croft called Mulecroft and 20 acres in the two Fields of Frome, including a croft called Lefdycourt with a dovehouse. Associated with the gentry were, of course, the clergy and a class of substantial merchants, acceptable as charter witnesses and therefore implying a degree of equality. Such were John the Fuller, Robert Smith, of Tytherington,

Roger the doctor, and the prepositus, or Abbey bailiff. Walter Isaac and Geoffrey Samuel were possibly of Jewish extraction.

The magisterial work of those gentlemen who held manorial courts was not heavy. No Court rolls survive for the main manor of Frome Branch but those for Frome Egford do. In 1314 the worst offences were the straying of animals, inevitable in the open field system with hedges few and far between. Geoffrey Pinnoc's sheep got in the lord's corn. German le Cornmonger let an animal into the lord's oats and John Braunch let two pigs into his garden. Clement Upehull and two others stacked the lord's oats so badly that the crop was lost. They were fined 40d each. In 1327 Richard Randolf drove two of his mares over a meadow at Garston and wrongly made a way there in the mowing season. Great gaggles of geese roamed the wastes and frequently strayed into the lusher meadows or cornfields. Large flocks of sheep were a feature of the countryside. There is much mention of the de Whatecombe family and their tenement. They were of some standing, witnesses to many charters, and may have had Bishop John de Drokensford of Bath and Wells as their guest, for he admitted a Rector of Porlock from Whetecumb-juxta-Frome in December, 1310.

As Lord of the Hundred, Nicholas Branch had more important privileges to maintain. Apart from his market, he claimed rights to stocks for the punishment of evil doers, ducking stool, a chair-like apparatus in which scolds and cheats could be carried about to receive the jeers of the crowd, or a ducking, waifs and strays and amercements, or fines for breaking the Assize of Bread and Ale of which commodities he fixed the price and tested the quality. The Ale-taster was an influential man, appointed annually at the Manor Court as John Waterman was for Egford in 1553. He was the successor to a long line of ale-tasters, for it is recorded at the Egford Court in 1314, that one John Smith sold his ale before sending for the taster. In 1280, Nicholas Branch successfully sued Gilbert de Clare, Earl of Gloucester, who had property at Keyford; the Prior of Maiden Bradley, who owned the Manor of Grandon, and Henry de Montfort, of Nunney, for refusing to pay the proper fines for breaches of the Assize of Bread and Ale which had taken place within the Hundred of Frome. He came off rather worse in another dispute the same year with Henry de Montfort, who (by virtue of a royal charter) had established a market at Nunney much to the annoyance of Nicholas, who believed that the goods which had been sold at his free market in Frome on Saturday were now being sold at Nunney on the Wednesday. Nicholas believed himself £20 out of pocket and the thought was a painful one. To the complaints of Nicholas, Henry replied with perfect logic that what was not disposed of at his market on Wednesday was taken and sold at Nicholas' on Saturday so that he had nothing to worry about. Nicholas must have been much taken with this reasoning for he rather lamely gave up the struggle.

For nearly 50 years Nicholas Branch was Lord of Frome and it is a pity that we do not know more about him. Either his spouse, Robergia was a later wife or he married late in life, for he was well over 60 when his son and heir Andrew was born in 1312, an event important enough to be inscribed in the chronicles of Longleat Priory. Nicholas was having a meal when John Wilchet was the first to announce the birth to him, an event which John remembered vividly more than 20 years later, as did Richard de Carswelheie and Thomas Southover, who were 'serving at the table before the said Nicholas' at the time. Andrew had an elder sister, Eleanor, who married Richard de Wynslade, of Gloucester. The couple were endowed with a handsome estate in Frome, Rodden and Marston Bigot valued at one eighth of a knight's fee. In 1318, now an old man, Nicholas began to put his affairs in order. He arranged the marriage of his infant son, with Joan, daughter of John de Kyngeston, and settled on the childish couple his estate: 'a messuage, 1 mill, 220 acres of land, 24 acres of meadow, 60 acres of wood, pasture for 18 oxen, 24 cows, 500 sheep and 60 pigs in Frome Braunche and Faleise'. John de

Kyngeston's involvement with the barons and their revolt against Edward II in 1322, defeated at the Battle of Boroughbridge, put the Branch estate in danger and Frome was threatened with seizure by the keeper of rebels' lands in Somerset. However, it was established that Kyngeston did not hold Frome himself but was only acting as Nicholas Branch's bailiff, so the keeper was ordered not to interfere with the Hundred of Frome or a pasture called Bolgh (Bollow). Nicholas, who enjoyed a long if not exactly tranquil retirement, died late in 1326, John de Kyngeston being granted the custody of the young Andrew during his minority, by the King on 26 November that year.

An interesting glimpse of Frome can be gleaned from the Exchequer Lay Subsidy, or tax roll, of 1327 when the people of Frome had to contribute to the cost of a royal marriage. There are 74 taxpayers (several names have been torn away) representing the richer inhabitants of the town, more than in Wells but apparently less rich as they paid £6 18s 2d against the £10 0s 6d paid by the citizens of Wells. Frome seems to have been on a par with Shepton Mallet (£6 9s 2d) and Bruton (£6 3s 9d). Nunney was in a different class with 38 taxpayers assessed at 51s 4d. The Frome list contains many names familiar from the local charters such as Portebref, Watecombe, Wilchet, Curseles, and Gryndenham and new ones such as Cable, Twynyho and Dunkerton, whose families were to become important in the town. John de Kyngeston, who paid 15d, was bailiff of the Hundred. It seems a small sum compared with some of the traders. Thomas la Taillour (tailor) paid 4s, John Boucher (butcher) 3s 6d, but William le Carpenter only sixpence. Blacksmiths and shoers of horses were no doubt in great demand and Nicholas le Ferrour (farrier) paid 2s. Adam and Thomas Vauntage were assessed at the substantial sum of 5s each. There were bakers, herdsmen, cooks and fishermen. Some local place names are mentioned. John Con is particularly said to be of Egford, and Walter Hyrebergh came from Tedbury. Two taxpayers came from Clink of whom Ralph 'de Cleneck' had to pay 3s. Others like William Dunkerton and Walter Sheftebury presumably came to Frome from further afield. That Frome was already engaged in the wool trade, which was to be its staple trade for centuries, is hinted at by the inclusion of Poleyn le Webbe (weaver) in the list, down for 2s. Firmer evidence of the establishment of the trade in the district is provided by three charters at Orchardleigh Park. In one of about 1300 John Fullo (the Fuller) grants a house in Orchardleigh to Henry de Cultura, and he witnesses another charter concerning the same village in 1306. In 1316, Thomas de Curseles granted Richard Body, fuller, 'one acre in the westfield of Fromebraunche against Whatecombe'. By 1349 Thomas, son of Luce le Webbe was of sufficient social standing and surplus wealth to endow, with others of the local gentry, the Lady Chapel in Frome Church. In the same year, Andrew Branch is recorded as owning a fulling mill. Frome, with its close connection with the woollen industry of the Cotswolds (through its association with Cirencester Abbey) and strategic situation between the sheep grazing uplands of the Mendips and Salisbury plain, was well placed to become a prosperous wool town and took full advantage of its opportunities.

From an early date the Abbot of Cirencester, overwhelmed with the burden of great possessions, rented out his land in Frome, including his capital messuage on what is now Christchurch Street East, which was in the possession of William son of Richard, Prepositus of Frome, before 1271. He in turn let it to Roger Medicus (the doctor) for 2s 5d a year with a right to fetch water, presumably from the spring above the church 'by a way leading from the court'. Roger let the Abbot have it back in return for a mark of silver and by 1342, even before the Black Death, he was leasing out the manorial demesne in return for a money rent. A charter at Longleat records how in that year, Abbot William leased for three years to Stephen Godrich, Chaplain, and Edward of Frome, all his manor and Court of Frome with crops and houses with permission to sell the hay on the small parcels of meadow. Stephen and Edward paid the Abbot

£24 a year for the privilege, plus 13 quarters of wheat to Gilbert Donkerton and Robert Combe, presumably his bailiffs. The abbot also reserved hay to feed his cattle at Frome and Langley, straw and chaff, the wages of four servants at Langley and a reaper at Frome, and an allowance for feeding the bailiffs' pigs. In addition, the lessees had to maintain the abbot's property, not only houses but also horses and carts, and give up everything at the end of their term, including the crops, as good as they found it.

There were easier ways to make a living. In 1341, Andrew Branch was ordered by the King to investigate 'divers persons' who 'went armed within the Hundred, wounding men, extorting from some of these by threats and fear of death, money and other things ...'. These turned out to be no ordinary thieves, but the whole de Merlaund family, of Orchardleigh, including Henry, and his two sons, Henry and William, and Edmund de Merlaund, the parson of Lullington. Andrew Branch was ordered to arrest and convey them to the Tower of London for trespass and 'confederations against the peace'.

Remains of mediaeval monastic buildings at Witham (Manor Farm) c1850, from a painting by W.W. Wheatley. (SAS)

ABOVE: Cheap Street in 1845 by W.W. Wheatley. (SA) LEFT: Originating in the Middle Ages: Broadway as it was c1900. RIGHT: Before the cutting of North Parade, the chief way out of the town to the north: Bridge Street, c1906

ABOVE: Palmer Street and Catherine Hill with Paul Street, formerly known as Behind the Hill, and showing Barton's shop and cottage, later cleared away and replaced by a public lavatory. (FM) LEFT: Elm had a manorial connection with Frome: the Old Rectory there was painted by W.W. Wheatley in 1846. (SA) RIGHT: Charter of William Branch, about 1270, granting the Manor of Frome Egford to his son, Thomas. It contains many field-names. (AD)

Interior of St John's showing the arcades, originally of c1300, but rebuilt by the Victorians. (FM) INSET: Mediaeval drain under Catherine Hill House, one of several still existing in Frome. (FM)

ABOVE LEFT: The Victorian screen and rood loft at St John's, a re-creation of the mediaeval splendour of the church. (FM) RIGHT: W.W. Wheatley's painting of the entrance to the 'Old Nunnery'; ancient home of the Twynyho family. It was taken down in 1849. (FM) CENTRE: The wooden doorway at Vallis, c1500, as it was in 1974. It has since collapsed (CB) BELOW LEFT: Part of the mediaeval house of the Cables at Grove Farm before the Second World War. RIGHT: Murtry Bridge, now disused but dating from c1400. (FM)

The Black Death

Frome's absorption in commerce was temporarily set back by the terrible interlude known as the Black Death. An outbreak of bubonic plague, it originated in China and gradually spread to the West. Traders brought it to Weymouth where many died, causing unease to the Bishop of Bath and Wells in his remote Manor House at Wiveliscombe; he warned his clergy of the cruel plague which 'as we have heard, has already begun to afflict the various coasts of the realm of England. We are struck by the greatest fear lest, which God forbid, the fell disease ravage any part of our diocese'. The Bishop's forebodings were all too justified. On 30 September, 1348, the plague appeared at Pendomer and soon struck the Deanery of Frome with particular virulence. Although there are no means of knowing how many, at least a third and perhaps a half of the total population of England died. One of the few indications of the plague's savagery is the number of institutions to benefices caused by the deaths of priests. In the Frome Deanery there were 34 institutions of clergy between January, 1348 and December, 1349, sufficient indication of mortality. There were three institutions at Cloford, three at Hardington, two at Elm, changes of priest at Pikewell, Whatley and Marston. Philip of Bath, Vicar of Frome, and John de Stratton, the Chaplain of St Katherine's, appear to have died. The Carthusian monks of Witham and Hinton Charterhouses petitioned the king for leave to hire labourers from outside their enclosures, as almost all their servants and retainers had died in the pestilence.

The plague tended to spare children and the aged, striking down the young and strong. Among those who were taken in their prime was Andrew Branch, the Lord of Frome, on 5 April 1349. Many Frome people accompanied him on that journey. The *inquisition post mortem*, the survey of the property of a tenant-in-chief taken after his death, recorded that: 'There are many dwellings in the Manor, formerly let, standing empty because most of the tenants are dead'. Andrew Branch left a son, Thomas who survived long enough to be contracted in marriage to a lady called Mary who later married John Gifford and was-provided for out of the Branch lands in Norfolk, besides 12s of rent 'issuing from the Manor and hundred of Frome in Selwode' in 1370. This is one of the first occasions on which the town was called Frome Selwood, its name until well into the 19th century and which has not entirely died out yet. The development is a strange one, since there are many places which have retained the names of their Norman lords unscathed many centuries after they had disappeared from the scene, and that Selwood Forest was growing less, rather than more important in the scheme of things at Frome. The two names are used interchangeably into the 15th century, the suffix Selwood gradually ousting Branch. Thomas Branch died in 1361, naturally without children, and the heir to Frome was his cousin, Stephen Wynslade, the son of Richard, who had died in 1352, and Eleanor Branch. Stephen had been born about 1328 and seems to have inherited the rude health of his grandfather, Nicholas Branch, living until 1405. He is described as a merchant, a curious and typically English development from the feudal pretensions of his grandfather.

Through his actions the inheritance of the Manor of Frome fell into a confusion that is a nightmare to unravel today and caused headaches to contemporaries.

Stephen Wynslade got into debt and granted the Manor of Frome to John Payne, a London armourer, for life. He borrowed from a wealthy magnate, Guy de Bryene, to whom by 1366 he owed £20,000, a staggering sum, in modern terms millions rather than thousands. Being unable to pay this sum, he granted de Bryene the Manor of Frome after John Payne's death. Payne died in 1376, when King Edward III promptly gave the Manor to his mistress, Alice Perers, who held it, as the disgruntled local jurors later told the royal officials, 'by what title or right the jurors know not'. After Mistress Perers was disgraced, Guy de Bryene recovered Frome and gave it to his son Philip. When Philip died, in 1387, his widow, Joan was given as her dower or widow's portion, a third part of the Manor of Frome Braunche including a suite at Vallis 'namely the high chamber over the gate with the Chapel within the Court of Faleys'. Among the land was Inhouk (near Innox Hill), a wood at Curchelle (Critchill), Cotelesassh, and mills called Nywmulle and Tristesmulle. Both Payne and de Bryene were troubled by the appearance of a mysterious figure named John Branch, the son of another John Branch, closely related to the manorial family (he describes himself as cousin and heir of Nicholas Branch), for as early as 1373 John Payne thought it politic to buy him off, while Philip de Bryene gave him the generous rent of 10 marks from the Manors of Faleys and Frome Branch, as well as two tunics with hoods of the same suit with furring to match the status of a yeoman. This John may have been an ancestor of William Braunche, connected with land at Mells in 1469. The name Branch Farm is still extant in that parish and perhaps forms a link with the old Lords of the Manor of Frome.

These changes and disputes caused problems at a lower level when it came to whose bailiff to obey or where to pay the rent. Life went on, however, and Frome recovered from the effects of the Black Death and prospered. Some went back to their bad old habits, like John de Wroxhele (probably from Wraxall in East Woodlands) who, on the Sunday after Midsummer 1368, stole a horse worth 18s from Adam Crockere at Wodeland, and then, to add insult to injury went on to 'Friggelstret' and purloined an even more valuable horse of Adam's, valued at 28s. Still not content, he doubled back to La Hampne (the area below Sandhill where East Woodlands Church now stands) and took Margery Davy's mare. John capped his cleverness by obtaining a royal pardon the next year.

Cirencester Abbey was an undying landlord which never overlooked its due. The rental of its Frome property, now in the Somerset Record Office and translated by Dr John Harvey, throws much light on the town in 1392. The old labour services to the Abbot had been partially replaced by money rents. Five streets are mentioned: Vicarestret, Twynhoestret (probably Gentle Street), Frigstret (Friggle Street), Cokkestret (Eagle Lane but which before the cutting of Bath Street went on further to enter the top of the Market Place; it was Cox Street in 1605 but later known as Back Lane; the Eagle was an inn), and Rolvestret. This was Blind House Lane, for it lay alongside the Abbot's barton (on the site of St John's School) and included three cottages at Le Corner with a way from the Abbot's Court. This fits perfectly with a lease of the Abbot's capital messuage before 1271, which mentions a way from its west corner (Cornura) to fetch water. Reading between the lines of the rental, a vivid picture presents itself of increasing activity and congestion round the Abbot's house. Alexander Webbe had converted a haybarn into a tenement there, while Andrew Smyth had made an entrance out of William Pilie's ground on the Abbot's soil, doubtless to make more room for his forge. Opposite, Andrew had a well, indispensable for the exercise of his trade. Next to Andrew's smithy was the great gate (*porta*) and Edward de Combe's house. The woollen industry was flourishing. Five fulling mills are mentioned, including one at Langley. William Laurance had a water mill beside his fulling mill. Henry Donkerton had 'rekks' (racks) for drying cloth 'next the churchyard on one side' and on '18 acres of land once of Peuerell on the hill'. Robert atte Purye also had racks. A John le Nappere is mentioned, whose name should indicate a connection with the woollen trade (one who raised the nap on cloth), but was in fact a farmer.

The labour services required seem exacting. In return for a house and a virgate of land (30 acres) John Bole was required to plough the lord's land for two days or, if he had no plough, to harrow for the same period with a beast. 'And shall mow the lord's meadow for 11 days before dinner and shall take each half-day of the lord's herbage as much as his ashpole may carry... And he shall make the lord's hay for two days and weed the lord's corn for one day and reap 11 1/2 acres of the lord's corn and gather and bind it and stack it...and he shall carry the lord's corn to the lord's barn with his cart and two beasts for 2 days...'. John was also required to carry the lord's letters (on the understanding that he should be given due warning) and sow his beans. Besides the holding there were some perks, including fare at the Abbot's board on various occasions. Perhaps in practice the hard edges of the contract were rubbed smooth. Among those holding tenements in Twynyhoestret (although not of the Abbot) was Sir William Stourton, the first appearance of this Wiltshire family in Frome. By the time he died in 1413, Sir William possessed seven houses and nine acres of land in Frome as well as 16s in rents and the valuable Somdyes meadow (beside the River Frome below Sunday's Hill Farm). The connection between the Stourtons and Frome was to last more than 300 years.

The deposition of Richard II and the succession of Henry IV (1399-1413) ushered in a period of civil war which lasted for most of his reign. It looks as if Richard had his partisans in Frome, among them Philip Bydyke, John Cayver (Keyford), John Cable, John Webbe, of Keyford, John Faber, the younger, and Hugh Milton who gathered together 'staves with heads of iron after the fashion of lances and other staves and axes.. .with heads of iron and lead newly made by men of Frome'. The news reached the new King—this was early in 1400—and for 'particular causes' laid before him he ordered the weapons sent to him in London on pain of £100 fine. Several other Frome men were indicted for treason: Richard Greylake, John Carreu, John Maret, Richard Tannere, John Beche, and Walter Penne, of Keyford. Beche, of Frome Selwode, was imprisoned in London but set free on the understanding that he would forfeit £1,000 if he went to Somerset before Easter, or sent any men thither with or .without letters 'in order to make unlawful assemblies in breach of the peace'. Beche survived his troubles, for he is mentioned as an overseer of the will of John Cable in 1408. The storm of Lollardism, a movement for reform of the Church led by John Wycliffe, shook the nation and was felt at Frome. The Somerset Lollards were strongest in Bristol but they had one follower in Frome named John Donne. Faced with the prospect of burning at the stake he recanted and received the royal pardon in 1414.

The Manorial question caused much heart burning among the rival claimants and appears to have reduced the royal clerks to total confusion, so much so that at one point (in 1407) they actually granted seizin,or legal possession, to Emmota Godeston, the daughter of John Payne, the armourer, who had only held the Manor for life. The Manor was frequently taken into the King's hands pending a decision. A more serious contender was Elizabeth Lovell, the niece of Philip de Bryene, but the matter was finally decided in favour of Elizabeth Wynslade, the daughter of Stephen the debtor and great-granddaughter of Nicholas Branch. She married Edmund Leversegge, or Leversedge as it came to be written, whose rugged Yorkshire name sounded strange to Somerset ears. Frome people had ample time to get used to it for the Leversedges remained among them for more than 300 years. It is difficult not to see them as violent, cantankerous, selfish, and untrustworthy, lacking that dignity and manliness which still faintly emanates from the memory of the Branch family. John Strachey picked up a local tradition in Frome in the 1730s that Leversedge 'came out of Lancashire & had been Steward to the family of Branch & married their daughter & heiress'. If there is any truth in the story his connection would have been with the Wynslades. He had property at Eastleach in Gloucestershire where he left land to the parish church.

The Leversedges began as they meant to go on. Edmund's father Hugh, who died in 1412, was a priest, and Edmund is first heard of in 1399 'averring threats' against John Murydene in Gloucester. He married Elizabeth Wynslade before 1404 and recovered the Manor of Frome in 1406, the King foregoing the personal homage due to him 'by reason of his having issue by Elizabeth'. The Lovells contested the decision bitterly and there was 'strife and discord' between them and Leversedge in 1410, but in the end they lost both the Manor and the £20,000. Edmund and Elizabeth had at least two children, Robert and Richard. However the Manor of Frome was not long enjoyed by Edmund Leversedge, who died fairly young in 1415 leaving to his children each 20 marks of silver, or chattels, a silver piece, a bowl, six silver spoons and a bed suitable to their rank. He did not forget Peter his servant, who received 20s. He also bequeathed 20s to the fabric of Frome Church, which was being enlarged and beautified in the early years of the 15th century. The nave was extended westwards by four bays and made lighter and more imposing by the addition of a clerestory, (the west face of the tower retains at the north-west angle the oversailing course for the high pitched roof of the 13th century nave), and the tower was raised in height and given a parapet and spire. St Andrew's Chapel was built to house a chantry in honour of St John the Baptist and in 1408 John Cable left £10 towards the rebuilding of the nave. He had already founded, with his neighbour John Twynyho, or John of Frome, the Chantry of St Nicholas (where the present Baptistry is situated in St John's Church) in the year of his death.-Most of this work the Victorians renewed, but an exquisite piscina (an ornamental drain for washing the sacred vessels) remains in St Andrew's Chapel. All this was financed, as in the Cotswolds, out of the profits of the wool trade. More evocative of the period than any work which remains at St John's is the splendid bridge across the Mells River at Murtry, now hidden by the modern road bridge outside the gates of Orchardleigh Park. Two massive arches remain, a third having been demolished, each supported by four handsome chamfered ribs of immense strength. As far as houses went, John Cable left £10 for building one for a tenant. He already had the wood ready for it at Keyford.

The Cables (the name is variously spelt Cable, Cabell or sometimes with a K) had a long and honourable connection with Frome. We first hear of them in 1305 when a John Cable held a messuage (house) in Keyford for life. He was probably the John Cable senior whose name is missing from the Lay Subsidy List of 1327, several names being lost. The Keyford seat of the family was Grove Farm (still brought to mind by Grove Lane and the Grove) where a rebus, or punning allusion to their name, a K and a bell in stained glass could be seen until the mansion, which had long been a farmhouse, was demolished in 1896. A mediaeval building associated with the house and described as a hall, survived in use as a dairy until after the Second World War. The wealth of the family is reflected in the will of John Cable, proved in 1408, which apart from the items already mentioned, made provision for a thousand masses for his soul, and 13 poor men to be clad in black or white garments to pray for his soul on the day of his burial, each holding a burning taper. His daughters, Lucy and Dionysia each received £40, a silver cup with cover and six silver spoons. The handsome sum of £6 was to be distributed to the poor at his funeral. The Twynyhos, who are thought to have taken their name from Twinhoe, near Wellow, were established in Frome by 1316 and lived at a house in Lower Keyford which, although largely destroyed in 1849, partially survives. The mansion was evidently in bad condition by 1740 when Strachey saw it: 'Ruinous walls, some Buildings of a Nunnery by tradition' as he noted. The house, divided into tenements, was known as the Old Nunnery, a fact which the Ordnance Survey by a happy, if puzzling transmutation, turned into the site of 'the monastery of St John the Baptist'. For this second supposition there is no foundation, but the name of the Old Nunnery has a respectable antiquity and deserves consideration. It is possible that the name arose from visits, accompanied by her nuns, of Margery Twynyho, Abbess of Shaftesbury (1496-1504), to her family there, or it may have arisen from the fact that in 1455, William Twynyho and Ankarette his wife received a Papal licence to have a portable altar in their house at Keyford. During the restoration of the house by Mr & Mrs James White in 1979, remains of late mediaeval wall paintings of high quality work showing Christ with St Peter and St Paul, which may have formed a suitable background to the altar, were discovered. The existence of these objects may have given the house a religious image in the public mind. But the most likely cause is the common identification of Gothic Architecture with church purposes when it may well be domestic. The two-light cusped window which survived at Keyford, until replaced by a copy, and the pointed doorways which still existed in 1849 may well have put people in mind of a religious building. The Twynyhos and Cables were close neighbours and friends. They founded the Chantry of St Nicholas together, shared the patronage and were buried together in its vaults. The will of William Twynyho, who died in 1412, is still extant and makes an interesting comparison with that of John Cable. The arrangements for his burial are much the same, but the benefactions on a much less generous scale—for instance the 13 poor people at the funeral had to make do with hose and shoes.

Such were two of the great families of Frome, quietly piling up treasure on earth, and making provision for their ease in the hereafter. There is no record of the Cables losing any of their silver spoons, but in 1442 John and William Bertelot, the one a husbandman or farmer, the other a labourer, and both of Frome, broke into the Manor House at Vallis and stole two silver jugs worth 12 marks, a silver pantener valued at 26s 8d and 14 marks in money. Robert Leversedge, the eldest son of Edmund and Elizabeth had now grown to manhood. He appears to have been still under age in 1430. He married Agnes Westbury, daughter of a wealthy judge with much property in that Wiltshire town as well as in Orchardleigh and Berkley. Much of this the Leversedges later inherited. When Agnes' father died in 1449 he left them his 'third best silver cup, 300 sheep, one sack of wool, and my second best horse' besides two gowns to Agnes personally. Robert had some quarrel with James, Earl of Ormond and Wiltshire, and Amice his wife (a relation) over property in Frome, and being unable to obtain satisfaction, took the law into his own hands and with a motley band of gentlemen, carpenters, weavers and shoemakers, 'armed with doublets, headpieces, battleaxes, swords and bows and arrows' entered 20 houses in Frome belonging to the Ormonds' son, James, and expelled him and his mother. To make sure they did not return, Robert 'constructed barriers within the bounds of the said town of Frome, and fortified and kept the same town for three days' not only keeping James and Amice from their property but shooting arrows, wounding and maltreating various folk, apparently friends and tenants of the Ormonds 'against the peace and in contempt of the Lord the King'. This was in 1444 and may have been the incident which caused Bishop Bekynton of Bath and Wells to appoint a commission early the following year 'to reconcile (something less than a reconsecration) the Church of Frome and the Churchyard thereof, which have been polluted by violent shedding of blood'. This breakdown of law and order, due to the weak government of Henry VI, was rapidly leading to the Wars of the Roses.

The general callousness which this long struggle bred amongst the nobility, and the contempt it engendered for normal legal processes, is well illustrated by a shocking incident in Frome. Ankarette Twynyho had in her widowhood become a lady-in-waiting to Isabell, Duchess of Clarence, the daughter of Warwick the Kingmaker and sister-in-law of Edward IV. Isabell died young and Ankarette retired to her Manor house at Keyford where she was 'of good name and fame'. Unfortunately, for reasons we cannot know, the unbalanced and ruthless widower, George, Duke of Clarence, became convinced that Ankarette had given Isabell 'a venomous drink of ale mixed with poison', evidently a slow one as the Duchess sickened in October and did not die until shortly before Christmas. The Duke brooded upon his wrongs until the following April, 1477, when he sent Richard Hyde 'accompanied with divers riotous and misgoverned persons in manner of war and insurrection' to seize Ankarette Twynyho. They arrived at Keyford at 'about 2 of the clock after noon' on 12 April and without any lawful authority broke and entered into the house 'with great fury and woodeness' carrying her off to Bath en route to Warwick, where the Duke resided. There a browbeaten jury condemned her to death and she was hanged on the gallows at Myton, an end for this gentle and religious Frome woman all the more terrible for being so unexpected. Her grandson, Roger Twynyho, who was later to be killed at the Battle of Blackheath fighting for Henry VII against the Cornish rebels, petitioned Parliament to set aside his grandmother's conviction, which it did. Before the year was out, retribution overtook the Duke. He, too, fell victim to a trumped up charge of being party to a plan to destroy the King by necromancy and astronomy, and according to contemporary rumour, was drowned in a butt of malmsey wine.

The West Front of St John's, rebuilt by Vicar Bennett in what he considered a pure mediaeval style. (FM) INSET: Alabaster figure, perhaps from a resurrection tier, found in Frome Churchyard and now in the Ashmolean Museum.

Winds of Change

The turbulent Robert Leversedge died in 1465, leaving three sons—William, 29 at the time of his father's death, John, and Edmund, the 'gay Leversedge' of Mrs Tuck's poem *Vallis Vale* who

'In the "Black Arts" forbidden lore,
Twas his delight, unseen to pore,
Till by the wizard teaching bold,
He sought dread secrets to unfold.'

There is no evidence to associate Edmund with witchcraft. Like so many of the Leversedges he lacked character and appears to have been a proud and frivolous young man, given to extravagant dress, doublets stuffed with wool and bolsters, short gowns and hose which perhaps exposed a well-turned leg and a shapely thigh, high bonnets, shoes with long 'pykes' and shoulder length hair. One day in 1465 'in the town of Frome' he was struck down by a pestilence and for three hours lay as if dead, his face 'black as any coal and my tongue...black as any pitch and thrust out of my mouth the length of half a foot'. His father had just died and he may have been particularly susceptible to depression. While in this trance his soul was taken on a journey through Hell. This concluded with a lecture from a good angel (apparently female) on his future conduct. It is particularly interesting to us for the angel's views on the vicar of Frome. The Vicar was Walter Osborne, who was also a prebendary of Wells, where the money was better and the living more comfortable. In these circumstances, Frome tended to be neglected, hence the views of the angel seem to reflect earthly rather than heavenly comment. Leversedge tells the angel: 'my curate, the vicar of the town where I dwell...can give me some counsel'. 'No,' replied the angel, 'he has no cunning (knowledge) thereto, nor is a priest about to keep any cure, but many a soul is departed from its body that stood in great peril through his default for which he shall answer before God. And God is greatly displeased with him in that his cure has not due teaching and information as they ought'. Leversedge (or his soul) replied that there were three other priests including the parish priest (presumably the curate as opposed to the vicar). The angel condemned them all as lacking in 'cunning', but finally agreed that he should see a priest at Westbury. (This is significant, as his mother, Agnes, had property at Westbury which Edmund later inherited). At the end of the ordeal, Leversedge's soul was returned to Frome Church where the angel delivered a parting broadside: 'Lo,' she exclaimed, 'the vicar is at Wells. It were better that he were here and kept his cure'.

Contrary to tradition, Edmund was not buried at Frome, but at Westbury where he died in 1496. The aisle north of the tower in Westbury Church was long known as the Leversedge Aisle. When Strachey visited Frome Church about 1740 he was shown the memento mori in the Lady Chapel and told it was in the monument of one of the Leversedge family 'who was supposed to be dead for 7 days but revived and lived many years'. The story has been much embroidered by various hands, but that it should have survived in oral tradition down to Strachey's day, shows that something strange did happen to Edmund Leversedge. The monument in St John's merely reflects the morbid obsession characteristic of the 15th century.

The style of the arches on the tomb chest suggests that it may commemorate Edmund's elder brother William who died in 1485. When Francis Thynne visited Frome Church from Longleat in the 1580s, he noticed a coat-of-arms upon it with the quarterings of various Westbury families, relations of William's mother.

Nothing evil is recorded of William Leversedge and he left a permanent mark on Frome by founding an almshouse of which the present Blue House is the direct consequence. The original foundation consisted of a chapel and hall with 12 chambers and was endowed with 4 1/2 acres of land. This was soon after William succeeded to his inheritance in 1465. The exact site is not recorded but it is unlikely to have been far from the 'Great Bridge of Frome' where it was standing in the 1650s. It seems that the income from the 41/2 acres was inadequate and the building fell into decay, for when in 1538 William Kyppinge.of Buckland, left six cows for the relief of the 'poure people' in the almshouse, he made the gift conditional on the profit being bestowed 'in mete and drynke and nott in reparacions'. William also embellished his manor house at Vallis, adding the great hall with a magnificent open timber roof divided into five bays, or compartments, by arched principals; massive purlins and curved windbraces supported the weight of the stone tiles which covered it. This roof has now almost collapsed and what remains is in the last stages of ruin and decrepitude, an irrevocable loss to Frome not only of one of its few mediaeval secular buildings but also one of outstanding quality, closely bound up with the history of the town.

In 1485, William died leaving a widow, Edith, and a son and heir, Edmund, who was 32 weeks old. The *inquisition post mortem* taken after his death mentions two profitable markets,one valued at £15 6s 8d, and the other at £24 13s ld. In addition, the profits of the Hundred were £8 a year, altogether enough money to live in some style. The baby Edmund, as a tenant-in-chief, became a ward of the King, who made Sir Robert Willoughby, Lord of Broke (probably a relation, Broke being near Westbury) his guardian. Willoughby de Broke delegated his duties to the child's uncle, Edmund Leversedge of the vision, until his death in 1496 when young Edmund was 11. However, his lordship did bestir himself to obtain from the Crown a confirmation and extension of the existing markets and fairs. There was a market at Frome in 1086 and the Saturday Market was being held in 1280, but until 1485 there is no reference to a second market day, which was taken without a by-your-leave. So on 24 June, 1494, Willoughby de Broke obtained a royal charter to hold markets 'at the said town of Frome Selwode and in other places and fields adjoining' on Wednesdays and Saturdays, and two yearly fairs, one on the feast of St Matthias the Apostle and the three days before it (24 February) and the other on the feast of St Mary Magdalen (22 July) and on the days before and after it. The first still existed as a cattle and cheese fair in 1785, the other died out before that date. This charter is in possession of the Frome Literary and Scientific Institution.

All this was good for trade and the merchants of Frome lived well, judged by their wills and the type of houses they favoured. The ideal is described in a lease of Walter Twynyho to John Taylor, alias Clarke, butcher, in 1500 of an empty plot near the end of 'le Chipstrete' (Cheap Street) on condition that he should build a house there with a hall, parlour and shop, cellar, and three chambers, within four years. Some of the houses in Cheap Street are among the oldest in Frome, not much later than this lease date. Although the frontage of the shops is picturesque, their antiquity is really brought home by a look behind them in Apple Alley, still a remarkable survival of old Frome. We hear little of the cloth trade at this time. A Matthew Grace (presumably a mistake for Craas, a notable Frome merchant family) made cloth in Frome in 1475, much of it carried to its destination by packhorse.

The rebellion of Perkin Warbeck in 1497 cost one Frome resident dear. Perkin, who claimed to be the Earl of Warwick, son of the ill-fated Duke of Clarence, and therefore rightful heir to the Crown that Henry VII had won from Perkin's 'uncle' Richard III, at Bosworth in 1485, landed in Cornwall and advanced into Somerset. How far he got beyond Taunton is not clear but he received some sort of succour from Thomas Champneys, of Frome, a member of the Orchardleigh family, who was fined for his pains £61 13s 4d. Champneys, who died in 1505, left a will in which he mentions his 'newe place in Frome...in which I dwell'. His brother Henry Champneys, died the following year leaving 'a capital messuage in Frome Selwode'. It may be that it was this house which was close to Sheppard's Barton (later leased to the Sheppard family and known as the Manor House of St Katherine's Hill) that became confused with St Katherine's Chapel. It was regarded as the capital messuage of the Champneys Manor at Frome Selwood. Like the Manor House at Keyford, it also seems to have pointed arches and a 'churchy' look. It is curious that both were dubbed in local parlance 'old nunneries'.

By the 1520s the standing of the church had fallen low. This was not because the monks and clergy were positively evil, but due to a malaise which had befallen them. There was some loose living. The Priory of Maiden Bradley was well-known in Frome, owning land at Waldyke and Grandon and maintaining a light burning before the altar in Frome Church. Of its Prior (officially celibate), Richard Layton reported to Thomas Cromwell, Henry Vlll's Vicar-General who masterminded the dissolution of the monasteries, that he had'but six children, and but one daughter married yet. His sons be tall men waiting on him: and he thanks God he never meddled with married women, but all with maidens and always married them right well. The Pope gave him licence sub plumbo (under his leaden bull or seal) to keep a whore'. Worse than immorality was the fact that the monasteries had ceased to work their estates or take much interest in them, leasing them out and living on their rents like landed gentry. Apart from leasing out the Rectorial Manor of Frome, Cirencester Abbey had even come to regard the advowson or appointment of the vicar as a piece of property like any other. Thomas Parker, who became Vicar of Frome in 1524, and had the advowson 'to hym before graunted by the abbot and his predecessor, John Taillor, had agreed that he should have 'all the Implements and Utensylles' at the Vicarage as well as 'beddinge Kychin staff as other to value of XL li'. Parker was understandably annoyed when another clergyman, Robert Bisse, took it all before he could reach his benefice. Lawyers found fault with obsolete legal privileges such as the right of sanctuary enjoyed by Witham Charterhouse, of which a Frome man, Richard Cabell, tried to avail himself only a few years before the dissolution, having killed a man by misadventure at Bishopstrow.

Nevertheless, St John's Church in Frome still attracted rich gifts and was decorated with exquisite carvings like the alabaster figure, probably from a Resurrection scene, which was found in the churchyard in 1870 and is now in the Ashmolean Museum, Oxford. The altar was rich in ornaments and precious vessels. Among the jewels were a great cross with Mary and John all gilt and set with white crystal stones, two great chalices all gilt, two great censors of silver parcel gilt and a silver ship, 'a pere of chandyll stecks parcel gilt', besides numerous cruets, pixes, and small chalices. However, these were no longer felt to be sacred and in 1528 John Twenow, Thomas Torrey and other 'gentlemen' 'between the hours of 2 and 6 of the clock after midnight', broke into the church by one of the north windows, opened the chest of church plate despite its three locks, and stole the contents, said to have been worth 300 marks. The jewels were sold to a Bristol merchant and never recovered. The burglary is reflected in the report of the Chantry Commissioners, who noted that there had been only one chalice between all the Chantries 'which the presentors say was stolen'.

The previous year Richard Cabell had restored the Chapel of St Nicholas. The great six-light window in the Baptistry, although renewed in the 1860s, is probably an exact copy of his work. Some of the heraldic glass with which they were filled survives, and is the oldest and most interesting in the church. The Cables married into the Leversedge family and were proud of their connection. The first shield shows the arms of Cable, *a horse salient argent, bridled or*, that is a silver horse standing upright and having a golden bridle. These arms impale, in Chief (in the top half) a leopard's mouth and, in base, a chevron between three dolphins embowed (bent) *argent*. This is a combination of the arms of the Branch family (the leopard's head) and those of Leversedge (the dolphins). These arms are repeated on the second shield without the intrusion of the Cable coat. In the third shield (in the next light) the Cable horse impales a golden candlestick whose top curls down to include two heads. This is a rebus of Branch. The heads have puzzled antiquaries, but they probably represent nothing more than an artistic conceit. In the final coat, Cable appears again impaling a rebus of their own name, a K and a bell.

In 1536, the assault on the monasteries began in earnest and three years later Cirencester Abbey was dissolved. As the lands of the Abbey in Frome were leased out, the amount of practical difference the dissolution made was probably small. One of the last acts of Abbot John has a defiant ring. On 3 December, 1538, he appointed Thomas Courte and John his son Receiver and Collector of the Rents in the Manor of Frome Selwode as well as Keeper of the Woods. The appointment was for life at a salary of £1 6s 8d, the rents to be paid to the Abbot twice a year. The Frome lands of the monastery and the advowson of St John's were granted to Henry Vlll's brother-in-law, Edward Seymour, Earl of Hertford, later Lord Protector and Duke of Somerset. He, in turn, alienated them to his secretary, Sir John Thynne, who also acquired the priory of Longleat from Sir John Horsey. Thynne survived the disgrace of his master, made Longleat his chief seat and built the magnificent mansion we know today. His descendants as Viscounts Weymouth and Marquesses of Bath, appointed the vicars of Frome until 1939, when the advowson was transferred to the Diocesan Board of Patronage.

Although the abbot was gone, religious change was slow. The Catholic ritual continued. Congregations were large and in 1548 there were 840 communicants. Leland saw the church in 1540 and commented that it was 'goodly large'. In 1545, Philip Jorden, the chantry priest of St Nicholas, could still look forward with confidence, leaving 7s 'to a discreet and honest priest to sing and say mass for my soul for one whole year in the parish church'. He also gave 20s 'to the reparations of my chantry'. With the accession of Edward VI two years later, the Protestant wind began to blow and the Chantries were dissolved. The last priests were John Lurpoole, of St Nicholas, John Fry, 'gentilman', of St Katherine's, George Burley, of St Andrew's, and Robert Gray, of Our Lady. They were pensioned off, and Vicar Phillips began to grapple with the Book of Common Prayer. Religious changes were reflected in the disappearance of 'Popish' ornaments. Much light is shed on this by the beginning of continuous church records in the shape of the first parish register (albeit a copy) which begins in 1558. The churchwardens' accounts, which start in 1567, when Thomas Wallis and Richard Johnson were churchwardens, provide a rich fund of local detail. Thomas Phillips, already curate in 1527 and in full charge of the parish by 1548, appears to have had a supple conscience, for he remained Vicar of Frome through all the religious changes of the time, finally resigning in 1564.

ABOVE: The Blue House, close to the site of the original almshouses founded by William Leversedge. The Guardhouse is on the right and the three entrances for the school, old women, and paupers, can be clearly seen. BELOW: Built close to the site of the mansion of the Chantry priest of St Andrew: the Chantry and the Hermitage, a view from the rear (FM)

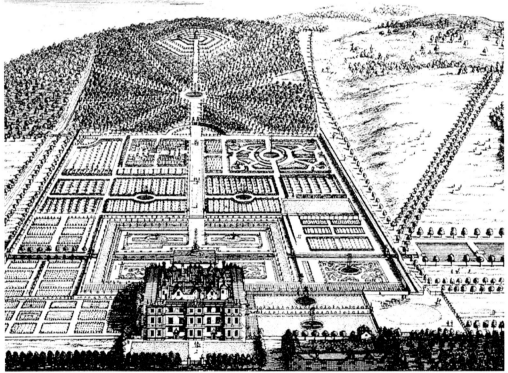

ABOVE: The great Bridge of Frome as it was in 1945, (FM) and BELOW: Longleat, c1700, the home of Sir John Thynne, A drawing by Leonard Knyff.

ABOVE LEFT: The ruins of Maiden Bradley Priory as they were in 1824. RIGHT: The fireplace at Vallis dating from the early 16th century. (CB) BELOW: The Old Church House—also dating back to the 16th century—once the home of Frome Museum. (T)

ABOVE- Where the Bell Inn once stood, Behind Town: Fairlawn House. (T)
BELOW: The Sun Inn, more than 200 years old. (FM)

Decline and Fall

We owe to John Leland, the King's antiquary, our first brief description of Frome. In about 1540 he travelled from Trowbridge by woody ground and pasture until 'I cam within a myle of it where is Champaine,' that is arable land. Leland crossed a stone bridge of five arches to enter the town, our first detailed reference to Frome Bridge, although Wallbridge is mentioned in the 13th Century. He mused on the source of the Frome which he considered came in two branches from Maiden Bradley and Hindon, observed that 'The Towne hath a metly good Market, and is set on the Clefe of a Stony Hille' and 'There be dyvers fayre stone Howses in the Towne that standythe most by Clothinge' and then went on to Nunney. Leland returned to Bath, passing through Frome again and 'about 2 Myles of(f) I cam to a Botome, where an othar Broke ran into Frome. And in this Botome dwell certayne good clothiars hauynge fayre Howsys and Tukkynge Myles (Mills)'. This may be a reference to Spring Gardens where the Mells River joins the Frome. If this seems a little close (it is barely a mile from Frome), the next point which fits the description, Shawford, where the Henham Brook falls into the river, appears to be too far and in any case was not as large as Spring Gardens.

It appears likely that one of the Chantry priests took in pupils and ran a school. For some years before 1570, a Crown grant of £5 13s 4d was paid to the Vicar in compensation for the endowments confiscated in 1548. In 1570, Hugh Kirk, who had succeeded Phillips as Vicar, was considered a worthy recipient of the money because he had been diligently teaching scholars at Frome free of charge, and because there was no other school near. Lacking evidence of its foundation by Edward VI, it became known as the Free Grammar School and for more than two centuries was run by the Vestry of St John's, who provided desks, furniture, books and buildings in return for the Crown grant. It probably always stood on the site in Vicarage Street, on glebe land, now occupied by St John's Hall, for when it was rebuilt in 1744, Samuel Bowden, a Frome physician, referred to the 'antient hall' which had previously been there. Apparently the Vicar soon found that he lacked the leisure to double as minister and teacher. In 1592 the burial of Thomas Chislet, school master (*scola moderator*) is recorded and the following year the churchwarden paid himself a shilling for going to Yeovil to fetch the money (the royal grant) for 'the scole of Frome.' Later, sums were paid out for glazing the premises.

The Leversedge family in the meantime had come within a hair's breadth of extinction. Young Edmund, orphaned at seven months, lived long enough to marry—Eleanor, the daughter of Sir Richard Wrotesley—and beget an heir before dying at the age of 24 in 1509. His son, Robert Posthumous Leversedge, born as his name implies after his father's death, was a true scion of his family, summoned to the Court of Star Chamber in 1531 and accused of being in Frome with six or seven 'evyll dyssposed persons in riotous maner arrayed that is to say with swerdes and stavys...'. They assaulted and beat one William Barker and his wife Alice and imprisoned them for three hours. Robert began the long decline of his family. He was arrested for debt in 1549, and when he died the following year, it was found that his estates were 'extended', the revenues held for the satisfaction of creditors, to a limit of 500 marks. He left a son, William, who came into his inheritance in difficult times. The Protestant Reformation had gained in momentum under Edward VI and seems to have been accepted, even welcomed in Frome, which so began its puritan and nonconformist tradition. It is significant that when the Duke of Northumberland sought to put his Protestant daughter-in-law, Lady Jane Grey, on the throne in place of the Catholic heir, Queen Mary, after the death of Edward VI, Lady Jane was proclaimed Queen at Frome on 19 July, 1553, Lord Stourton being much taken to task for not preventing it when his house was not 'past V miles' from the town. It had been otherwise in the West, where in Devon the people rose in favour of the Catholic faith only to be savagely suppressed by the Government forces. An example was made at Frome where one of the prisoners was hanged, drawn and quartered, payment being made for the execution, for irons, for wood (needed for a fire to burn the entrails) and a pan and trivet (three-legged support for the cauldron) to seethe the limbs.

This stern duty was supervised by Sir John Thynne, the Lord of Longleat. The arrival of this alert and dominant man on the Frome scene put the Leversedge family further into the shade. He was not only patron of St John's Church (and he took his duties seriously, agreeing that he and his heirs should be responsible for the upkeep of the Chancel in 1574) and Lord of the Manor of West Woodlands, but also bought up the lands of the Chantries of St Andrew and St Katherine. Frome St Andrew's, as it was called, included the mansion house with a garden adjoining the churchyard, and a ruinous house (much Frome property was so described) in Small Street where William Gentle lived with Alice his wife and his daughter, Agnes. Small Street was an alias for Hunger Lane, with which the Gentles became indelibly associated and to which they gave their name. They appear to have been small farmers and what made them notable is unclear. The St Katherine's property was also ruinous, very much so, and the canny Sir John lost no time in selling it for £400 in 1563 to Richard West, yeoman, the son of that Alice West who had leased Frome Rectory and the home farm from the Abbot of Cirencester. The sale included 'the capital messuage or the mansion house of the said free chapel' situated where the Old Presbytery now stands, described by West in his will made in 1580 as 'the old building of my mansion house at St Catherine's'. It contained a parlour with a chamber over it and an adjoining buttery, which illustrates the modest dimensions of the mediaeval mansion before rich Englishmen decided that they must live in vast houses.

Sir John kept voluminous and detailed terriers of his estates written up by his servants in a noble hand. One remains at Longleat House for West Woodlands, dated around 1568. In Frome the market had always been the dominant factor and the town had expanded untidily along the routes that led to it. The Thynne survey mentions four roads to and from it: Hunger Lane and Vicarage Street, already mentioned in the Middle Ages, and Rook (spelled Roke) Lane and Stony Street, which appear for the first time. Before the cutting of Bath Street in 1810, the route of Rook Lane lay further to the West, emerging in Behind Town (as Christchurch St East and West was originally known) by Rook Lane House. The area between Vicarage Street and Christchurch Street East was called Above Towne, later altered to Upintown, a usage which survived into the 19th century. There is also mention of New Street, a curious name, as it was in the heart of the country east of Tytherington, where a water-grist mill called Claybridge stood on the banks of the Frome. The town had expanded southwards up the hill since the Middle Ages, but was, as today, very much a country town, the thatched and tiled houses being associated with assorted gardens, closes, bartons, barns, stables, and sometimes separate kitchens. The size of some can be gauged by the description of that of Morrice Merrick: 'one cotage new builded containing 1 feeld tyled (that is one bay or division of building) abutting south and east upon the Churchyard containing in length XII foote and a half and in breadth VIII foote adjoyning to the tenement of John, Lord Sturton.' The rent was 16d and six chickens.

The Church House was a substantial tiled structure of four bays. This stood on the right (entering from Bath Street) of St John's Churchyard, where the war memorial now is, and should not be confused with the building on Church Steps now called the Old Church House, which was the original Angel Inn. The Church House was probably already an inn where Church Ales were held as fund raising events. It was later known, with others, as the Bell. There was an interesting tenancy in Tytherington where Thomas Lodvyn, instead of paying rent, had to find his lord 'as much lyme as shal be sufficient for the building at Longleat' as long as he or Sir John Thynne lived. Among the dwellings listed is 'a mansion house of timber building thatched' called Riperd Place with two mills underneath it, one an undershot grist mill, the other a tucking mill. This was the now vanished Friggle Street Mill near Mill Lane on the edge of Corsley parish. Barne Mill, near the present Rodden Mill Farm, also housed both tucking and grist mills. It was leased to John Hutchyns in 1531, a long lease indeed, as he was still living in 1611, aged 97. A later Longleat survey (about 1580) mentions by name our first Frome public house 'one messuage being an Inne called Ye Bell.' It was a tiled house run by Joan Alford and had a stable, barton, and garden. This was not in the churchyard, but in Christchurch Street East where Fairlawn House now stands. So countrified were its surroundings that the Bell had a close of pasture and a pigsty 'before ye doore of ye said messuage'.

Much of Sir John's property lay in the Royal Forest of Selwood, which was still a potent force. The deer were browsing over St Algar's Farm as they had done for centuries, much to the dismay of its new owner, Sir John, who expressed the wish that 'the deere myght not have such pleasure there'. His bailiff, Mr Walker immediately put '8 poor yewes' in to mind the deer. John Hales, the Forest ranger, ordered them to be impounded or driven out with dogs. Each time Hales drove them out, Walker put them back again. Finally, when Walker and some companions were at St Algar's on 27 April, 1563, 'looking upon the herd of deere,' Hales came up and berated them saying: 'we dyd more than we could justifye and that we ought nott to follow nor trouble the game' and after 'more stowt words' told Walker point blank that 'no shepe should be kept there and I assured him that both the shepe should go there except (unless) by Law he could put them thence and I also wold walke wheare and wyche way I list in that ground having charge there, make of it what he could, and therapon belyke he went to Mr Horner (the Verderer) and told him what was said to him and medyatly he sent Henry Hales to putt forth the shepe agayn and so he dyd, and we, seeing that, went and putt them in before his face agayn, and then Hales went to your (Sir John Thynne's) hedgers and commanded them in the Queynes name to cutt no fryth (underwood) without the hedges and also to make as well the medow hedges low and without eny beard as also all the outside with many threatening woordes, as the hedgers told me'.

The landowners appear to have got round the Forest Laws, so much so that in 1613, the Surveyor-General of the King's woods south of the Trent brought an action against several of them, including the Leversedges and Sir Thomas Thynne, for despoiling the Forest. According to the indictment they had felled 3,000 timber trees as well as much underwood and 'armes of trees', hunted, chased and killed the royal deer, depastured, eaten and spoilt the grass with their oxen, kine, horses, geese and swine, and built 60 cottages or 'poore houses of habitation' which they had filled with ' diverse severall poore vagrant and idle persons for certayne yearlie rente and other considerations'. The surveyor estimated the damage at £5,000 and more.

By the mid-16th century, the authority of the manorial and hundred Courts had been much reduced and local government came to reside in a combination of Vestry, Justices of the Peace and Constables appointed at the Court of the Lord of the Manor. In 1583 the vestrymen sign themselves for the first time. These were important people responsible for the maintenance of the Church, and most of the town government. Among other things they had to keep dogs out of the church and keep down 'noysome vermin'. They paid 2d for snakes and hedgehogs, a shilling for foxes and badgers, and Is 9d for otters. It was also their job to organise the perambulations of the parish bounds. These were taken seriously, a fine of 2s being imposed for non-attendance. However, the beaters stopped so frequently for refreshments at the pubs with which Frome was so liberally endowed, that the perambulations became a burden on the parish, and expenses had to be severely limited. Yet another function was to levy the church rates and the records of these throw much light on the development of Frome. In 1596, 124 people were rated including three 'gentlemen'. Mr Edmund Leversedge, Squire, heads the list, paying 30s. By 1616, the chief centres of population are Clynke, Wallmarshe, Caterne Hill, Frome towne, and Chepstrete, Cayford, and East and West Woodlands. The vestrymen of 1583 were, appropriately, the representatives of church and state, the vicar, William Chubb, and the Lord of the Manor, Edmund Leversedge, supported by Thomas Wallis and William Chapman.

The 16th century was a time when old names began to vanish and new ones appear, such as Smiths, Whitchurchs, and Jessers, followed by the Whittock family, which gave its name to Whittox Lane, and the Iveleafs. The Smiths, wealthy clothiers, bought the land of the Chantry of St Mary in 1607. This became known as 'the manor of the Chauntery' and they built the fine gabled house now known as Stonewall Manor. After the Smiths migrated to Combe Hay, it was let to a Widow Austin and long known as Austin's House. The Smiths were also associated with Rook Lane House. The family estate in Frome was sold in 1776 after John Smith died, leaving debts of more than £16,000. The Jessers were also clothiers and first appear in 1602. They had a fulling mill and dye-houses at Welshmill, but became grand and cultured and later supplied the town with schoolmasters and attorneys. The Whitchurchs, established in the town by 1573, were linen drapers, and may have come from Shawford where a John Whitchurch had a fulling mill in 1516, or from Rode where Whitchurchs were numerous. They were leading figures in the town for more than 200 years, their success crowned with the shrievalty of Somerset and the lordship of the Manor of Nunney.

On the other hand the Cables and the Twynyhos left the town in which they had been so prominent. Christopher Twynyho, the nephew of Roger, killed at Blackheath, had married Edith Bampfylde, the heiress ofTurnworth in Dorset, where his descendants flourished until 1773. His brother Edward, however, got into debt and Edward's son, Thomas Twynyho sold the Manor of Great Keyford in 1585 to Clement Fysher for £400. Likewise, Richard Cable, the son of Richard who had beautified the Chapel of St Nicholas in Frome Church, married an heiress from Buckfastleigh in Devon in 1581 and vanished from the Frome scene. Some idea of the wealth of this family is given by an *inquisition post mortem* held after the death of Joan, widow of John Cable, in 1506. Their possessions included a messuage with a close of meadow in Great Keyford, a fulling mill, three messuages, five tofts, a dovecote, 250 acres of land, 30 acres of meadow 60 acres of pasture and 120 acres of wood in Wanstrow, Cranmore, Great Keyford and East Woodlands. By 1740, when John Strachey was collecting his notes on Frome, this great holding had dwindled to one little house. The Cable property passed by marriage to the Fownes family and when Richard Fownes died in 1744, leaving debts of £7,400, a private Act of Parliament had to be passed to sell his estates. Much Frome property is listed including 'all that Wear (Weir) and Walls adjoining to (Fromewater) near the Town Mills' but nothing in Keyford unless it be that 'One acre of Land lying in Ryals near Keyford's Elm'. The Cables appear to have been represented in Frome by a junior line, probably descended from a younger son of Joan. They came down in the world and the last of them, John Cabbel, who sold his property in the Trinity Area in 1736, was a carpenter and joiner.

Nicholas Cabell, who married Rachel Hooper at St John's on 15 November, 1697, was representative of the senior branch who had moved to Warminster. The American branch of the family, who erected the brass in the Baptistry to the memory of John Cable and which gives the wrong date for the foundation of the Chantry (1517 instead of 1408), are descended from Nicholas's son, William. Descendants still feel a strong tie with the home of their ancestors and in 1979 members of the Cabell Family Association returned, and were entertained at an animated tea party in Frome Vicarage.

In 1569, faced with the threat of invasion from Spain, the government of Queen Elizabeth ordered a census (Certificate of Musters) taken of available men and arms in England. The parish of Frome mustered 68 able men as against 23 in Bath. Not surprisingly, considering the violent tradition of his family, William Leversedge of Vallis was able to produce two pairs of almain rivets (armour for the back, breast and thighs), two corselets, a gelding for a light horseman fully equipped, a murrion, (a type of high helmet) and an 'harquebut', a musket fired from a forked rest. Richard West, of St Catherine's,was the only other Frome notable to have such valuable weapons. He provided one coat of plate, presumably an old fashioned suit of armour, a corselet, and a bill, sword, and dagger. The stockpile of armour held by the tithing was somewhat sparse and old-fashioned. It included a jack (a suit of mail), a bow and a sheaf of arrows, and a 'skull', a close-fitting iron helmet which fitted the top of the head. Among the able men were 27 archers. Archery was still compulsory, and the Butts in Frome still recall where the ablemen practised, as verified by several leases which survive, identifying property by its nearness to the place where the Butts formerly stood. In about 1628 William Hackett repaired the Butts at a cost of 40s, when he was waywarden or parish officer in charge of the highways. The men of Frome, however, preferred to play at unlawful games like bowls and football instead of practising with their bows, and he does not appear to have recovered his expenditure from the Vestry, but Quarter Sessions awarded him 20s. About the same date Richard Style, a young Frome yeoman, was had up for using a hand gun instead of practising archery. He realised the bow had had its day. At the time of the muster, archers were outnumbered by 29 billmen and eight pikemen. There was one light horseman, Thomas Perce, and a solitary 'gonner', Thomas Stedes, guns still being the prerogative of either the rich or the military. Frome historian, J.O. Lewis wrote in 1943 of the names recorded: 'Sixty years ago, 75 per cent of those names were still known in the town and its neighbourhood'. Amongst the many familiar names are: A'Court, Eggell, Norfolke, Baylye, Styell, Chinnock, Hipstone, George, and Hales.

We hear little of William Leversedge, who, had the invasion materialised, would have led this motley force. He married Grace Roynon and seems to have lived quietly at Vallis, retrenching his finances and breeding sons of whom he had seven besides two daughters. When he died in 1582, he left his younger sons £100 each and £40 a year—ample to live on. His second son, Arthur was left a house in Egford called Maggesons, plus a black gelding. Roger Leversedge got a bay gelding without a house. William also remembered his god-daughter, Anne Horner, who was to receive a jewel of gold, and his servants. His cook received £5 and Agnes Burges, his 'old woman', 40s. Vallis now came into the hands of his eldest son Edmund who, by his first wife Margaret Morgan (died 1587), had a son Robert (1584-1667). Edmund's second wife Elizabeth joined with her husband and step-son in a whirl of extravagance, violence, and exploitation of Edmund's rights and dues as Lord Royal of the Hundred, which brought ruin on the family. The disputes between the Leversedges and their neighbours fill acres of parchment in Chancery and Star Chamber. In one of the most serious cases, they were indicted of conspiring to murder Walter Coles, and having gathered together in their usual manner 'riotously ..armed and arrayed with swords, daggers, and guns', drove away 15 of his beasts 'and shutt them up into a close courte walled about with a high wall and with a strong door fast locked'. Other accusations were that they pulled down Simon Coles' hedges and made a common way through his grounds, and built cottages on the commons and wastes in which they 'planted' poor people, an accusation already levelled by the King's surveyor of woods. The Leversedges accused Walter Coles of having murdered a woman called Margery Foxbery. Francis Leversedge, Edmund's brother, said the Coles were 'troublesome persons and common disturbers of their neighbours'. Edmund and Robert Leversedge, on the other hand, were gentlemen of good and quiet behaviour. In another case, William Thicke complained that he and his father had bought the office of bailiff of the Hundred (it was a valuable office: Thicke claimed that he paid £200 for it plus a rent of £22 a year) but when he tried to collect the tolls at the time of the fair, Edmund Leversedge's henchmen 'all armed with bills, staves, swords, daggers and naked knives did in most rude and rioutous manner' set upon Thicke and his father, declaring them deposed. One Richard Tucker thrust at Thicke with a knife. The clamour and outcry at the fair were so great that the Constable arrived, but was unable to assert his authority. The Thickes departed 'for fear of our lives'. However, Thicke's complaint to Star Chamber was successful for he is mentioned as Bailiff in 1612, eleven years later.

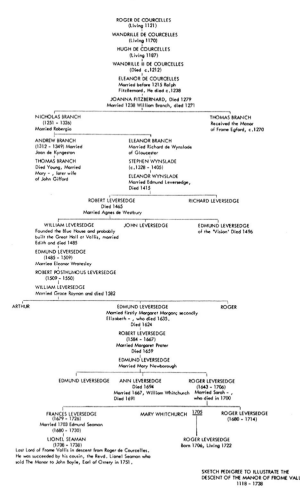

SKETCH PEDIGREE TO ILLUSTRATE THE
DESCENT OF THE MANOR OF FROME VALLIS
1118 - 1738

This case of Leversedge versus Coles was in 1608. We know much less about the event, which took place in 1606, described in a 17th century document at Longleat as a felony committed by Elizabeth Leversedge and three of her servants. Prebendary W.E. Daniel in *The Street-Names of Frome*, speaks of 'a murderous assault' at the Egford entrance to Vallis Manor. Mrs Tuck in her poem *Vallis Vale*, imagines a dispute at Court and a duel between Edmund and his opponent 'with one furious, deadly blow, The other laid his victim low.' However, Edmund lived until 1624. The actual circumstances are still shrouded in mystery, but the fact remains that the Leversedges were tried and found guilty, presumably of a murder, and risked the forfeiture of their lands if not their lives. Edmund Leversedge invoked the help of the Knight Marshal, Sir Thomas Vavasour, who obtained a pardon for them from James I, no doubt at a heavy price, and defrayed all the charges and expenses of the operation. In return, Edmund and his son Robert had to make over to Vavasour their manor of East Woodlands, the most lucrative part of their estate. He in turn sold it in 1611 for £2,450 to Sir Thomas Thynne, of Longleat. The Leversedges reserved the rents for their lives and Edmund was to have forty cart loads of wood for his fire each year, and sufficient timber to repair his dwelling house at Vallis during his lifetime. Neither their prestige nor their finances ever recovered from the blow.

ABOVE LEFT: One of the more substantial houses of St Katherine's Manor: 7 Trinity Street c1900. RIGHT: Conservative headquarters on the corner of Christchurch Street West and Bath Street, taken down for road widening. OPPOSITE: Palmer Street has changed beyond recognition since 1900, when it contained handsome houses like this one on the corner of Bath Street, which was demolished to make way for BELOW: the Co-op building in 1921. (EK)

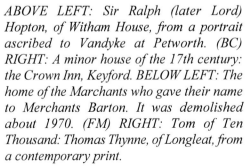

ABOVE LEFT: Sir Ralph (later Lord) Hopton, of Witham House, from a portrait ascribed to Vandyke at Petworth. (BC) RIGHT: A minor house of the 17th century: the Crown Inn, Keyford. BELOW LEFT: The home of the Marchants who gave their name to Merchants Barton. It was demolished about 1970. (FM) RIGHT: Tom of Ten Thousand: Thomas Thynne, of Longleat, from a contemporary print.

King Monmouth

If the Leversedges felt the pinch in the first years of the 17th century, so did Frome. As early as 1575, Peter Blackborough, a Frome clothier, in a petition to the Privy Council against the abuses of the aulnagers, the officials responsible for sealing cloths as being the correct weight and width, had complained that trade was declining and the workers impoverished. In 1622, the inhabitants petitioned Quarter Sessions praying for some relief for the poor who were 'much impoverished by reason of the decay of clothing'. The response of the Justices of the Peace was niggardly. They ordered that one pound a quarter be paid to the Constable of Frome 'to be distributed according as need shall require'. By 1631, Frome was said to be 'very poor' and to have 6,506 inhabitants, mostly clothiers, weavers, and spinners. The depression also hit Bath and the other clothing towns. This situation made the Almshouse all the more necessary, and Edmund and Robert Leversedge, despite their financial difficulties, appear to have rebuilt it at this time, for it is described as 'lately erected' when in 1621 they conveyed it to trustees, on condition that they allowed 12 poor men or women, born, or to be born in Frome, to live there and enjoy the gardens and the profits from its endowment of 4½ acres. This house stood on the roadside between the present Blue House and the Blue Boar Inn. When in 1644, Robert Leversedge conveyed the premises to new trustees, they are described as containing a hall, and 12 chambers, a chapel 'and two gardens thereunto adjoining' lying north and south of the Almshouse. This was before the coming of the Blue Boar, which was not built by Theophilius Lacey until 1691. One of the original trustees was Robert Smith, the clothier, who died in 1625. He had already made his pile by the time the depression struck and besides his lands and houses was able to leave his five children £200 each. Robert, the eldest son, received his 'greatest silver saulte, gilted, and my greatest silver bowl'. Each of his weavers was given 12d and each 'spinster', 6d apiece, a welcome bonus.

Frome was no backwater, generally receiving and welcoming visitors, and helping them on their way. So the churchwardens gave Is 6d to a soldier 'that cum out of Turkie' in 1616 and, in 1627, a similar sum 'to three distressed Irish gentlewomen travelling to London'. Two years before, they had received less welcome visitors in the shape of the Phillips family, who had fled from an outbreak of the plague in London and brought the infection with them. The authorities acted with speed and decision and shut Phillips, his wife and child up in a remote house, keeping 'good guard and watche' so that they should not escape and spread the plague. Here the unfortunate family all died. The operation cost the parish £8, which the justices allowed them to recover, by levying a rate 'if they find the said Towne of Froome to be burdened with poor as is alleged'. The house in question, at the corner of Grove Lane and Marston Road, became known as Plaguey House but is now demolished.

During the great Civil War between Charles I and his Parliament (1642 to 1649), the sympathies of Frome, with its population of Puritan weavers and spinners, lay with Parliament. Frome got away lightly, for the war raged all about. Sir Ralph Hopton, who became Commander of the Royal forces in the West, lived nearby and was a well-known figure in Frome, having recruited local troops when he took part in the Thirty Years War in Germany in the 1620's. His seat, Witham House, was twice besieged by the enemy. Woodhouse Castle, a seat of the Arundell family, just over the parish boundary of Frome in Horningsham, was garrisoned for Parliament and taken by the notorious Royalist commander, Sir Francis Doddington. In retaliation for the execution of some of the King's Irish soldiers, Doddington hanged 12 of the prisoners from a giant oak (later cut down and made into desks) and buried them under a mound known as Clothiers' grave. One of the prisoners threatened the Anglican parson that he would 'stick in his skirts' for reading the Book of Common Prayer, upon which Doddington struck the man so many blows on the head and with such force that he broke his skull. The man then 'fell into a sword', from which he had no sooner recovered, than he was picked out to be hanged. This was in 1644. The previous year there had been a fierce skirmish at Leigh-on-Mendip, when in a daring night raid, a Parliamentary troop had charged out of the morning mist and caught a Royalist unit in its beds. Despite the activities of the modern 'Sealed Knot', who enacted an engagement some years ago, there was no fight at Frome. Hopton's Cornish troops were in the town in July 1643, on their way to secure the bridge at Bradford-on-Avon, and it was probably on this occasion that they slept in St John's Church, the Churchwardens paying out 2s afterwards for it to be cleaned. The following year, King Charles I was in the vicinity, travelling from Bath to Mells where he stayed in the 'faire large house' of Sir John Horner, a Parliamentarian. On 18 July, 1644, the Prince of Wales, later Charles II, dined with Lord Hopton at Witham before joining the general rendez-vous of the Royalist army at Nunney the next day. It is unlikely that Hugh Clarke, described in the Churchwardens' accounts as 'killed in ye field' in 1648, when they received 6s 8d for his burial in the church, was a victim of military operations.

The Puritans tightened their grip on St John's, taking down the painted glass in 1643 and replacing the Book of Common Prayer with the new Directory of Public Worship, as Parliament directed. It was not, however, until 1651 that the Churchwardens got round to removing the symbol of Royal power from the Church, paying 'Will Crease for defasing and white lyming the late Kinge's Arms in ye church, and for lyme, 2s'. Charles I had been beheaded and the monarchy abolished two years before. Disillusion with the new regime had been swift and in 1649 there were riots in Frome against the high taxes imposed, demonstrators described as not 'the scum and malignants of the town,but such as have faithfully served the parliament'. The breakdown of authority inevitable during the war had caused problems. The £4 a year due to the Almshouse from the County Hospital money was five years in arrears by 1648. Some had taken advantage of the troubles, and in 1647 three of the most respectable merchants of Frome, William Ivyleaf, Thomas Wimpew, and Henry Marchant were found guilty of furnishing unlicensed alesellers with malt. Hence they were forbidden to make malt for three years. The proliferation of these houses accounted for such incidents as when Matthew Eyres and his brother were beaten up by men from East and West Woodlands, who were 'high in drink', playing cards and fiddling all day in disguised habits—a 'mumming' party that went wrong. Henry Marchant gave his name to Merchants Barton. His house, demolished about 1970, was on the corner of Church Street. The entrance to Saxonvale now goes over the site. The fine plaster ceiling which bore Henry's initials and those of his wife, Joan Walters, was removed to the Priory Barn, Bradford-on-Avon, Frome being unwilling or unable to find a home for it. What Frome thought of Oliver Cromwell does not transpire, but on his death in 1658 his son Richard was proclaimed Lord Protector in Frome with some style by Abraham Selfe the Bailiff, and Richard Wayland, his drummer, five shillings being spent on beer and 3s 6d on a bonfire.

Robert Leversedge had supported the King, albeit reluctantly according to his own testimony. He had settled down since those days when he and his father had turned Frome upside down. Before 1614 he married Margaret, daughter of George Prater, of Nunney Castle, an event probably commemorated by the fine wrought-iron screen decorated with the arms of Leversedge impaling Prater, which he caused to be erected in the Leversedge Lady Chapel in St John's. Alas, the Victorians threw it out and the screen is now in the Victoria and Albert Museum. The couple appear in an unattractive light in the will of Mrs Leversedge's father, proved in 1623: 'As for my daughter Leversedge,' he writes, 'I think she and her companye have spent me more by a great deale then I did promise with her, wherefore I must entreat them to live of themselves which I hope they will be able to do shortly'. In his old age, Robert saw another man add to the endowment of the Leversedge Almshouses. This was Alexander Stafford (1562-1652), a Frome man who had made a fortune in London and left £30 a year to the Almshouse. Of this £28 was to be given to 14 poor old women (this allowed the original foundation to be increased by two), one pound was to go to the Vicar of Frome for two sermons, 10s on gloves for the vicar and trustees, and the last 10s on a dinner for them at their yearly account, or annual general meeting.

We have Robert Leversedge's own account of his activities during the Civil War, no doubt tailored to suit the times. He had been classed as a 'delinquent', (supporters of the King were so described) and in 1646, approached the Committee for Compounding, for permission to compound, or pay a lump sum in return for his estates. He told the committee that 'living under the power of the King's army, he was constrained to execute a commission from Oxford (where Charles I had his headquarters) for the raising of contribution money and regulating His Majesty's garrison within the said county through fear of loss of his estate though he did little therein practical...' He declared that he held no public office—'nor am even a counsellor'—was not 'Popishly affected', and had taken the Covenant to establish Presbyterianism. Yet his estates had been sequestrated and he had been imprisoned. The Committee judged his rents from Frome to be worth £40, the demesne of Vallis £91, in addition to which he had £15 worth of goods and £20 a year from the Manor of East Woodlands for life. Robert was fined £480. He was also assessed for war expenses at £300,but in consideration of his debts, this was later reduced to £140 and paid by 1652. This pusillanimous gentleman lived to be more than 80, dying in 1667, having witnessed the King come into his own again in 1660, when the Frome churchwardens, bowing to political reality, paid a painter £2 10s for 'setting up the Kinge's Armes' in the Church, and John Rich Is 4d for making clean the place where they were to be put. They also spent a pound on cleaning the highways when the King rode through the town. Robert was succeeded by his son, Edmund, who married Mary Newborough, of Berkley, and was the ninth generation of his family to live at Vallis.

The Restoration brought a decided change of atmosphere in Frome. This was not least because the calvinistic Dr John Humfry, minister at St John's, was unable to subscribe to the new Act of Uniformity, and resigned in order to lead a dissenting meeting in Rook Lane. Dr Joseph Glanvill, who succeeded him, a man of original thought and 'of a quick, warm, spruce, gay fancy', became a chaplain to Charles II and was elected a Fellow of the newly founded Royal Society. He was a considerable preacher by the hour, and a noted authority on witchcraft, the results of his investigations being gathered together and published in a book called *Saducismus Triumphatus*, or *Full and Plain Evidence concerning Witches and apparitions*. Today it makes amusing reading. There is much in it about a coven of witches at Brewham, less than 10 miles from Frome, to whom the Devil 'appeared a little man in black clothes to whom all made obeisance, and the little man put his hand on his hat, saying, How do ye? speaking low but big'. He would then vanish leaving a smell of brimstone, but sometimes return at five in the morning in the likeness of a hedge-hog and suck the left breast of a witch. The Doctor's zeal and brilliance could not be contained in Frome and in 1666 he moved on to a larger stage as Rector of Bath. However, he kept the Frome living until 1672 when he exchanged it with Richard Jenkins, the Rector of Street. Jenkins had the distinction of performing the marriage ceremony of Thomas Thynne, of Longleat, his patron and Lord of the West Woodlands Manor, to Lady Ogle, née Percy, heiress to the vast possessions of the Earls of Northumberland. The marriage took place in London or Richmond on 14 July, 1681 and as Jenkins read the words 'with all my worldly goods I thee endow,' Thynne laid 100 gold guineas 'with some silver mixed therewith' on the prayer book from which Jenkins was reading. Lady Ogle took the money from the book, put it in her handkerchief and kept it. The following year Thynne, known as Tom of Ten Thousand (such being his supposed annual income) was assassinated in Pall Mall, and Longleat with its Frome estates passed to his cousin, Thomas, almost immediately created Viscount Weymouth.

Frome appears to have accepted political and religious change without too much heartburning, once the dissenters had split from the Church of England. Perhaps the well-known Frome apathy played its part. The churchwardens in the midst of paying Richard Drap 'for keeping ye boys in order about ye church' and 'setting a Ewetree and railing him', found time to ring a dutiful peal when the Rye House plot against Charles II was discovered in 1683. But puritan feelings still ran deep. The accession of the Catholic James II aroused misgivings and when the news reached Frome that James, Duke of Monmouth, the illegitimate but protestant son of Charles II, had landed at Lyme Regis, it struck a responsive chord. Monmouth advanced by Taunton and Shepton Mallet on Bristol, but was repulsed by the King's forces at Keynsham and fell back to Norton St Philip, where he is said to have slept at the George Inn. Here some of the Royal troops came up with them, but were repulsed in a sharp encounter. Excitement gripped the neighbourhood. Two to three thousand people assembled around Westbury and Warminster. At Longleat a group of labourers, creating the great Dutch garden for Lord Weymouth, left to join the rebels and the steward feared that 'Myles the Warrener is gone over to the rebels. I can never find him at home of late'. Two chests of Longleat plate were discreetly dispatched to Salisbury. After all was over Edward Hill, steward of the Marston estate, congratulated his mistress, the Countess of Orrery, that only one of her tenants had defected. In Frome, Robert Smith, the Constable, posted up Monmouth's proclamation as King in the Market Place, at the pillory where the Boyle Cross now stands. With the country in arms arid the Duke's army so near, it must have seemed safe to do so.

Smith had not counted on the resolution of the Royalist commander at Warminster, the Earl of Pembroke. On hearing the news, he at once rode to Frome with 160 horse, and 36 musketeers mounted behind them. As they approached the town they heard great shouting and beating of drums. This was on 25 June, 1685, while Monmouth and his army were still at Norton, but there were already rebels enough armed with muskets, pikes, pistols and scythes. Pembroke marched into Frome at the head of his musketeers, followed by the horsemen. At first it seemed that there would be resistance, for as the Earl 'came in at the gate', a rebel fired at him, telling everyone else to do so when he reached a particular spot. However, their courage failed them and 'in a moment' the rebels threw down their arms and fled to the other end of the town. Pembroke tore down Monmouth's declaration. The Constable had the misfortune to be on hand, and was made to write out a declaration that Monmouth was a traitor, which was put up in the same place. Pembroke was unable to garrison Frome and, having carried out a striking show of authority, withdrew into Wiltshire taking Smith with him, a prisoner. The Earl lost no time in reporting to Lord Sunderland, the Secretary of State, who conveyed the news to James II. The King, as Sunderland reported to Pembroke in a letter of 30 June, 'is very well satisfied with what your Lordship has done and as to the Constable of Frome His Majestie thinks it fitt that ... hee bee forthwith hanged as he deserves'. There is no evidence that this Royal mandate was carried out and the name of a Robert Smith appears amongst those deported.

At daybreak on 28 June, the Duke of Monmouth and his army entered Frome. They were up to their knees in dirt, having spent a miserable and sodden night. According to a tradition which goes back at least to 1774, the Duke stayed at the tall stone house with transome windows and gabled roof in Cork Street, called in honour of the noble guest once housed within its walls, Monmouth Chambers. Dating from soon after 1600, it still retains, in an advanced state of dilapidation, a fine plaster ceiling which testifies to its ancient standing. Alternative suggestions, although rather later in origin, are that he stayed at a house in Stony Street or at an older dwelling which was taken down when Thomas Bunn's father built the house, which was (and is) called Monmouth House, in Cork Street in the 1760s. Wherever he stayed, Monmouth was disappointed, for he had great expectations of the town, but these did not materialise. Perhaps Pembroke's raid had bred caution. Instead of new recruits, many deserted, encouraged by James II's proclamation offering deserters a free pardon. Monmouth received bad news here. The Earl of Argyll, who had landed in Scotland in support of Monmouth, had been defeated. He pondered on whether or not he and his officers should ride to a sea-port and return to Holland, but decided to fight on. He rode round the town and was seen by the Longleat steward, Mr Allen, who noted that his supporters 'called him King as confidently as if he had the crown on his head'; Allen had heard that the rebels in Frome numbered 30,000, 'but if there be so many, the greatest part was asleep whilst I was there'.

What discipline there had been in Monmouth's army had vanished by the time it reached Frome. George Roberts, when gathering material for his two volume 1844 life of the Duke, picked up several local traditions. One concerned a man called Toop at Oldford. He was brewing ale when Monmouth's men came down from Norton, and immediately hid his money, a considerable sum, among the grains in the mash-tub. The rebels ransacked the house, took what they pleased and said they must have the grains for their horses. Toop, with great quickness of mind, begged a skilletful for his pig. This was agreed, and Toop scooped up the money with the grains and carried it to a safer place. He told the story and laughed about outwitting them for many years. Monmouth's cavalry were said to have been billeted at the Old Nunnery in Lower Keyford, the Twynyho mansion, and to have turned the oak tables upside down, put hay between the legs and ranged their horses round to feed in place of rack and manger. When the Duke retired to Frome, outposts were stationed on Roddenbury Hill and on Marston Hill near Bull's Quarr, with sentries placed at strategic intervals in between to give warning of surprise. One sentry saw a snake and drew his sword to kill it. The glitter of the blade in the sun alarmed the next sentry, and ultimately threw the party on Marston Hill into confusion, expecting a surprise attack but uncertain of its direction. Another tradition speaks darkly of robberies and murders at Cottle's Oak, a grimmer record, like the tale passed down at Norton St Philip, that the wounded from the skirmish there crawled away and died in the standing corn, where their bodies were later found by the reapers.

Monmouth stayed too long in Frome in a state of fear and indecision, before deciding on the retreat that eventually led to defeat at Sedgemoor and his execution on Tower Hill. He left on 30 June for Shepton Mallet. Many deserted him here, abandoning their horses in the woods to be less conspicuous. The local landowners hoped to make some profit from these mounts and searched their coppices for them. Lady Orrery's steward only found one, which he ruefully told her the woodmen had dubbed the Monmouth mare. Lord Faversham, the King's commander, entered Frome on 1 July. He can hardly have looked favourably on the town which had proclaimed Monmouth, and when so many clothworkers were included in the rebel army. Many prisoners were confined in the parish church which, as usual, had to be cleaned after their stay. After the Bloody Assize at which the rebels were tried and sentenced, 12 were executed on Gibbet Hill at Frome. The names do not seem to belong to Frome. The quarters of the victims were hanged as a frightful warning, above Gorehedge between the Butts and Keyford where the fire station now stands, but which until less than 20 years ago was the site of the Unicorn, a popular pub on a busy junction. From these prosaic facts a chilling story arose: that the heads of the rebels were placed on the hedge there, which subsequently became covered in blood, a robust tale worth recording. However, all this happened in 1685 and 200 years earlier Henry Vincent,'countryman' of Keyford left 6s 8d towards the repair of the way 'which lies by a hedge called Gore Hegge'. The name derives from the Old English *gara*, meaning the triangular piece of land which lay at the meeting of the roads here. It shows clearly on old maps and is discernible even today after the total rebuilding of the area.

Rook Lane House: one of the several residences of the Smith family, wealthy clothiers, and later the home of Elizabeth Rowe. (CB)

ABOVE: Monmouth Chambers in Cork Street where the Duke of Monmouth is believed to have stayed during his visit to Frome renovated by Mrs Dorothy Brown. (CB) INSET: A once stately house in Cork Street, now gutted and ruinous. (CB) LEFT: Houses demolished in that part of Gorehedge known as Greenhill Place, not far from where the quarters of the Monmouth rebels were hanged . (FM)

ABOVE: Nunney Castle in 1733, with the house built by the Whitchurch family beside it, from an engraving by the Buck brothers. CENTRE LEFT: A late 17th century fireplace in situ at Vallis, and RIGHT: also at Vallis—a 17th century barn adjoining the Manor House. (FM) CENTRE: Thomas Ken, Bishop of Bath and Wells, from a portrait at Longleat. BELOW: The Iron Gates in its great days before the Second World War, with large garden and many trees. (FM)

Hail and Farewell

Following the Monmouth rebellion, Frome entered a period of great prosperity, based on an upsurge in the wool trade. The great clothier families were able to delegate more of their business to minions and, while keeping their fingers on the pulse, devote time to the pursuit of learning, the acquisition of culture, and the design of houses. They held high office in the county and were on terms of equality with peers of the Realm. There was not much in the way of local competition. Lord Weymouth of Longleat was an old man and rarely came to Frome. The Leversedges, the Lords of Vallis, were coming to the end of their time. Although they were prolific, the children tended to die in infancy. Edmund Leversedge had three sons of whom the eldest, the last Edmund of Vallis, died before his father in 1676. All his children died young and the succession passed to his brother, Roger (1643-1706). Three of Roger's sons also died young, leaving as representatives of the Leversedge family, his surviving children Roger, born in 1680, and Frances (1679-1726). The declining family was now being taken over by those of the robust merchants. Two Leversedge daughters married into the Bull family, clothiers of Hall House,one of whom has a handsome monument in St John's, among the few clothiers to do so. Frances Leversedge married Edmund Seaman, a mercer, or dealer in wool, while Roger, the young heir of Vallis, married Mary Whitchurch. It must have been galling to Roger Leversedge the elder that, when the county wanted a High Sheriff from Frome in 1690, it was not he, the Lord of the Hundred, who was chosen, but William Whitchurch, a wealthy linendraper.

The Leversedges were not to disappear without an undignified squabble about property. Roger the elder 'was taken very sick at his dwelling house at Vallis' in November, 1705, and seems to have been persuaded by his daughter, Frances Seaman, to make a new will in which he left 'my manor of Frome Selwood, alias Frome Vallis, alias Frome Braunch and the Hundred of Frome and the Market of Frome Selwood with all the tolls, customs and duties belonging out of my fair of Frome Selwood together with my messuage and farm of Vallis' to his son Roger for life only, and then to Frances Seaman and her family. Roger contested this hotly, especially as just before his father died on 23 February, 1706, young Roger's wife gave birth to a son, Roger. It was all in vain, for this Roger, the 12th and last of the Leversedges of Vallis, died as a young man. With the death of Roger the elder in 1714, the Manor of Frome passed to the Seamans. It was not inappropriate in this seat of commerce that its Lord should be a mercer. A collateral branch survived and was represented in 1851 by an Edmund Leversedge, who was master of Nunney School. He retained 'the family coat-of-arms engraved on an ancient seal'. His son went to New Zealand, where descendants remain.

Beside the busy merchants and professional people of Frome, the Leversedge family seemed a mediaeval relic. Another link with the past went, when in 1696, Lord Stourton sold his Frome property, which the family had held since before 1392, to Lord Weymouth. The Champneys of Orchardleigh, had sold or leased much of their Frome property, but contrived to take a keen interest in their right to appoint the sexton at St John's, a perquisite which carried valuable emoluments and which they had possessed since before 1590, by virtue of their Manor of Frome Selwood. Their heir in title, Arthur Duckworth Esquire, still makes the appointment today. Generally, the merchants and attorneys had things their own way unless they went too far, as when, in the reign of William III, they tried to secure a Charter of incorporation, which would have crowned their dignity by making Frome a self-governing borough with a Mayor and burgesses. However, Lord Weymouth thought it would adversely affect his rights as Lord of the Manor of West Woodlands and nipped the scheme in the bud. Frome had to wait until 1974 for a Mayor, but only to gain in pomp what it lost in power. Some of these families tended to become landed gentry. William Whitchurch, who had been High Sheriff, bought the Manor of Nunney in 1700 and built the exquisite house beside the castle, now again known as the Manor House. One of the Jessers in later years became Lord of the Manor of Little Corsley in Wiltshire.

The Sheppard family ultimately went this way, but in that period stuck closely to Frome. They came from Tytherington (not the Wiltshire one, but the Frome hamlet) and can be first identified in the town in 1642, when Edward Sheppard leased part of the Champneys possessions here. His son, John is described in various deeds as a cardboardmaker. He manufactured the leather or wooden foundation, formerly set with teasels but latterly with wire teeth, used to comb wool to open and mix it before spinning. As the wool industry expanded cardmakers became prominent; so did wiredrawers, the men who put the teeth in the cards. As late as 1761 there was an inn at Garston Stile known as the Wyredrawers Arms, perhaps that shown on the 1774 plan of Frome as the Horse and Groom. In 1662 John Sheppard leased the Manor House of St Katherine's Hill from the Champneys family and bought the adjoining ground called Rack Close (Sheppard's Barton by 1750),on which High Street and Wine Street were later to rise. At some point, he switched trades and became a maltster. His will was proved in 1675. He left £1,913 13s Od. John Sheppard, his second son, is the first of the family to be described as a clothier, from which trade came its fame and fortune. He lived on Catherine Hill, but his sons William and John moved to the Iron Gates, the fine house in King Street which, after years of neglect, has just been restored. It first appears under this name in the Church rates in 1696, which must be shortly after it was built. Early in Queen Anne's reign an extension, with a characteristic shell-hood over the door, was added at right angles to it. This is known as the Court House. There is no record of courts being held there, although tradition suggests that prisoners were held in the basement. This may refer to the period between 1745 and 1750 when William Sheppard and his brother 'bullhead Jack' were magistrates, much resented for their severity, and may have interviewed prisoners there. Another example of clothiers' trappings is Melrose House in Whittox Lane, a lopsided structure which looks as if half of it has been hived away. It was in fact built like this, a style not uncommon in Somerset at the time. Melrose House had transome windows with stone cross bars and mullions when it was built. These were later blocked or converted to more fashionable sashes.

Less imposing but even more elegant are 14-16 Willow Vale, again the homes of clothiers. Their doors, with shell-hoods, are raised up on a *piano nobile* above a basement and they have sophisticated windows, tall and slim, surrounded by fashionable bolection moulding and capped with a classical architectural device known as a pulvinated frieze. They make an interesting comparison with the fine, but more bucolic Market House in Bridge Street. Further good examples of early 18 th century stone carving are the coupled doorways of the Packhorse Inn, with their serpentine pediments enclosing urns (replaced by copies 1983).

The Georgian house beside Rook Lane Chapel was built by Colonel Richard Prater. He had sold the Manor of Nunney to the Whitchurch family, partly because he was in debt, partly to escape association with his brother-in-law, Thomas Pickfatt, a man of 'no competency or fortune, and of mean parentage and education' whom his sister had married without the consent of her family. Prater lived here in some style until his death in 1748, having extensive stables behind the house, where the old Victoria Baths used to stand. A more dedicated public servant than Colonel Prater was James Wickham, an attorney or solicitor, who died in 1727. He came of an ancient family, originally of Bristol, but later of Horsington in Somerset, which claimed kinship with William of Wykeham, the founder of Winchester College and New College, Oxford, and used the motto 'manners mayketh man'. James Wickham came to Frome as a young man and married into the Whitchurch family. He was well established by 1693-97, during which period he paid a shilling for a seat in St John's. Wickham served as churchwarden for seven years and, while in office in 1720, launched a public subscription for rebuilding the almshouse and providing a new school, made necessary by the increasing population. It was a measure of Wickham's powers of persuasion that many dissenters subscribed to his appeal. He became treasurer, and his determination and capability brought the matter to a successful conclusion. The school was functioning by 1723, when six boys were put out as apprentices. Eventually there were 29 scholars. The boys wore long blue coats with brass buttons, from which fact the building became known as the Blue House. Enough money was subscribed to erect, not only the almshouse and school, but also a guardhouse, or lock-up, walls and two arches over the river. The total cost was £1,401 8s 9d, which included £12 8s 0d for the figures of 'Nancy Guy and Billy Ball, up against the Blue School Wall', carved by William Langley, and £22 for a clock made by James Clark.

A mason called Richard Coombes was the main contractor. Among the materials used were nearly 48,000 laths and 12,290 feet of oak board. Architecturally, the building was a curious mixture with a centre which would not have been out of place in London, having four large arched windows and an imposing doorcase like that of Rook Lane Chapel. The whole was framed by rusticated quoins (stones at the outside angles) and a cornice, and crowned by a cupola. So far so good. Unfortunately, the recessed wings on each side represented a regression into an uninspired style, with plain mullioned windows and ugly chimney stacks sited amazingly in the centre of the front facades. The centre block was used by the school, which did not close until 1921, the boys in their distinctive uniforms being a familiar sight in the town. The south wing was used by the 'blue women' of Alexander Stafford's foundation, who received a blue gown every two years and five shillings a week. Women paupers inhabited the north wing and were also given gowns. James Wickham was succeeded in his practice by his nephew James. Later a Wickham took one of the Cruttwell family of Bath as a partner. A Cruttwell married a Daniel, also from Bath, and so was born the well-known Frome firm of Daniel and Cruttwell (now FDC Law), representing the business James Wickham founded nearly 300 years ago.

Others pursued less worthy aims. The remote backwaters of East and West Woodlands became notorious for the coining of false money called Woodland groats (a coin equal to 4d) and for clipping, or paring, the genuine coin of the Realm. In the time of William III (1689-1702), says John Strachey, the trade in clipping and coining was so on the increase 'that it hath been affirmed the very children were taught to be assistant in rubbing ye edges of ye dipt money and the artificers so secure that they scarce shut their doors when they were about their employment and the Tythingman either confederate or afraid of them'. Finally, in 1693 a party of soldiers quartered at Frome were ordered to attack a gang of these coiners at a place called Salmons or Seaman's house, where they withstood a veritable siege, in which a coiner was killed and others taken and executed. Strachey says that this broke the knot, but as late as 1714 one Nicholas Andrews, of Frome, was hanged on Oldford Hill with two Wiltshire men 'for counterfeiting Her Majesties Coyne'. The parish register also records the burial of two Frome men convicted of High Treason in 1697. They were Abraham Vaters and William Vaters, executed at Wells and Salisbury respectively. In 1683, one Stevens was tried at Wells but evidently brought back to Frome for execution, the churchwardens giving the workmen 3s 6d when his scaffold was set up, and 2s 6d 'for takinge of it downe and carryinge it away'. It was probably to bring a civilising element into what was evidently a remote and brutalised part of the parish of Frome, that Lord Weymouth built East Woodlands Church on Sandhill in 1712. The builder was James Pope, who also erected Rook Lane Chapel. Lord Weymouth died in 1714 and it was some years before the building was completed. For the time being it was a chapel of ease to Frome, and it was not until 1856 that a vicarage was built for a resident cleric.

The most notable event of this period was the burial of Thomas Ken, the saintly Bishop of Bath and Wells. In 1688, he refused to break his oath of allegiance to James II by taking one to William III. He and some of his colleagues were deprived of their sees in 1691 and came to be known as the non-jurors. On his deprivation, his friend, Lord Weymouth, offered him a home at Longleat where he spent 20 years in study and quiet devotion. He died there on March 19, 1711, after a long illness, having told his doctor that he had 'no reason to be afraid of dying'. Ken willed that he be interred in the churchyard of the nearest parish of his former diocese and was buried at Frome at daybreak on March 21, twelve poor men carrying his coffin to the grave outside the chancel and close to the high altar.

Let other thoughts where'ere I roam
Ne'er from my memory cancel,
The coffin-fashioned tomb at Frome,
That lies behind the chancel.

A basket-work where bars are bent,
Iron instead of osier,
And shaped above that represent
A mitre and a crosier

(Monckton Milnes)

The rough iron grating is probably contemporary, for it is mentioned by Bishop Pococke in a journal of his travels through England in 1754. Ken bequeathed 'my little patin and chalice gilt to the parish where I am buried for the use of sick persons who desire the Holy Sacrament'. They are still among the most treasured possessions of St John's.

Among Ken's friends at Frome was Elizabeth Rowe, soon to become the town's most famous resident and a poet of international repute. She was born in 1674, at Ilchester according to her biographer, Henry Grove, but in the view of the Earl of Orrery (who knew her well and later owned the house), at Maed House, Egford, which her father, Walter Singer, a prosperous wool merchant, leased from the Leversedge family. Singer had married Elizabeth Portnell, of Ilchester, and had property there, but the family appear to have returned to live in Frome about 1688. Elizabeth Rowe wrote her major works in the town and until she married Nicholas Rowe, a classics scholar and 'most amiable youth' in 1710, Maed House was her home and the neighbouring Vallis Vale her favourite haunt. Until quarrying destroyed it in the 19th century, a cave was pointed out there as Mrs Rowe's grotto.

From early childhood Elizabeth showed a love of literature and art which was fostered by her father, 'in whom parental affection conspired with a penetrating discernment', and by her mother who hired a master to teach her drawing. At the age of 12, some of her verses came into the possession of Henry Thynne, son of Lord Weymouth. He undertook to teach her French and Italian. There began a literary relationship with the Thynne family which lasted until her death. Elizabeth became a close friend of Henry's daughter, Frances, later Countess of Hertford and Duchess of Somerset. This lady became a notable blue-stocking, expecially interested in the relation of Nature to God, and who enjoyed pious meditations amid sylvan solitudes. Although younger, her influence on Elizabeth Rowe was profound. Bishop Ken was naturally introduced to this prodigy. He encouraged her love of poetry and steered it into religious channels. They shared a delight in solemn music and Ken would pay a weekly visit to Elizabeth at Egford. Ken's influence is revealed in her reluctance to publish and her once famous Devout Exercises of the Heart only appeared in print after her death.

Elizabeth Rowe was not always a gloomy mystic. She was an attractive woman possessing 'a large measure of the charms of her sex. She was of a moderate stature, her hair of a fine auburn colour, and her eyes of a darkish grey inclining to blue, and full of fire. Her complexion was exquisitely fair and a natural rosy blush glowed in her cheeks. She spoke gracefully, and her voice was exceedingly sweet...' When asked during a childish illness if she were not prepared to die, she replied frankly that she was not. Marriage to her much younger husband (she was 36, he 22) kept her earthbound: 'Dissolv'd in bliss and melting in thy arms,I loose the relish of celestial charms'. The death of Nicholas Rowe in 1715 cut these ties and strengthened the ascetic side of her nature. Elizabeth was persuaded to dedicate her talents to God and to virtue. She retired to Rook Lane House which she shared first with her father until he died in 1719, and then with the Congregational pastor of Rook Lane Chapel, John Bowden. Here the once gay young woman devoted herself to the contemplation of death, to seeking the spirit of divinity through Nature, to writing solemn verses, and to acts of piety and benevolence. In 1726, she told Lady Hertford: 'I am certainly dead and buried according to your notions of life, interred in the silence and obscurity of a country retreat'. She achieved in her lifetime European renown, and corresponded with some of the leading literary figures of the day, but nothing would induce her to leave Frome, and Lady Hertford commented: 'She will not go from Frome but to her grave'.

So it proved. Elizabeth Rowe died in her bedroom at Rook Lane House of an apopletic fit on 20 February, 1737, an event commemorated in 1974, the tercentenary of her birth, by a plaque on the house erected by the Frome Society for Local Study. She was buried in Rook Lane Chapel. By her own wish there was no ceremony and no tombstone. A memorial erected later has disappeared in the general destruction by vandals which has overtaken all the monuments in Rook Lane. Elizabeth Rowe's poetry is not easily obtainable, as the last edition of her works was in 1796. Much has a timeless verity, much is full of grandeur, and there is often a moving poignancy. Some reflects that latent sense of fun which she never quite lost, characterised by a charming little poem, *On an unsuccessful attempt to draw Lord Boyle's picture*. Lord Boyle; later Earl of Orrery, was her neighbour at Marston House:

> In vain with mimic skill, my pencil tries
> To paint the life that sparkles in those eyes
> What art, what rules of symmetry can trace
> That air of wit, that bloom, and modest grace?
> What soft degrees of shade or light express
> The inward worth those speaking looks confess?
> 'Tis more than beauty here that charms the sight
> And gives our minds an elegant delight
> Were virtue seen by mortal eyes, she'd wear
> Those peaceful smiles, and that engaging air.

ABOVE LEFT: John, Lord Boyle, afterwards Earl of Cork and Orrery, to whom Elizabeth Rowe wrote a poem. From a portrait by Charles Jervis. (GHB) RIGHT: Frances Thynne, Countess of Hertford - a friend of Mrs Rowe. CENTRE LEFT: Frome prided itself on stately doorways. This was the entrance to Griffin House in Palmer Street, now rebuilt. RIGHT: The Guardhouse, on the bridge erected in 1724 and demolished in 1965. BELOW: From left to right: a view of Bath Street showing Colonel Prater's house formerly in Rook Lane; Melrose House from a pen and ink sketch heightened with white, by David Grapes; (FM) the home of Elizabeth Rowe, now called Maed House, as it was in 1840; (FM) and East Woodlands Church, built by Lord Weymouth to civilise the Woodlands. (FM)

ABOVE: Rook Lane Chapel, one of the finest nonconformist places of worship in the West of England. CENTRE: Selwood Farm, probably built by John Selwood. LEFT: Castle House, rare for Frome in having a Georgian brick front imposed on a 17th century house. (CB)

Grand Hive of Schism

The Act of Uniformity in 1662, imposing the Book of Common Prayer, laid the foundation stone of nonconformity in Frome. Dissent flourished and fragmented. Frome became notorious among nonconformists for its splits and quarrels and to Anglicans loomed large and offensive, 'a grand hive of schism,' as Rev Stephen Hyde Cassan, curate of Frome, 1819-21, described it. Bishop Pococke, in Frome in 1754, noted: 'There are a great number of dissenters here of all sorts'. Dr Humfry, minister at St John's, although a moderate and 'a man of ability and scrupulous conscience' was unable to accept the Act and was consequently 'ejected' from the living. He and his friends took to meeting in a room in Rook Lane and so founded the Rook Lane Congregation. The Five Mile Act of 1665, which forbade former ministers to live within that distance of the parishes they had once served, drove Dr Humfry from Frome and he left for London where he died in his 99th year in 1719. Fortunately, the Act which forced Dr Humfry out, brought in Rev Richard Alleine, a noted preacher and theologian, who had been ejected from Batcombe. The congregation now met in Rook Lane House in a room made available by Robert Smith (he died in 1703 after which the Smiths ceased to live there). Alleine got on well with the Anglican vicar, Rev Richard Jenkins and when he died in 1681 was buried in St John's, the Vicar preaching his funeral sermon. This was a rare example of amity for when Alleine's congregation moved to Sheppard's Barton, their meeting house was destroyed by the mob.

In 1689, the Act of Toleration allowed dissenters to possess their own licensed meeting houses. Nonconformity had the support of wealthy merchant families, such as the Sheppards, Jessers and Smiths, while it was Joseph Ivyleaf who provided the Congregationalists with their new chapel in Sheppard's Barton after their first one was destroyed. However, it was the Smith family, who in 1706 leased them the 70 ft square plot on which Rook Lane Chapel was to rise. A condition of the 200 year lease was that 'a good substantial house, costing £300, at the least' should be built. No expense was spared and James Pope, the builder, created one of the finest nonconformist chapels in the West of England. It was deliberately domestic in character, its unusual grandeur perhaps reflecting the influence of the Smith family. Although rectangular in shape, its facade was in the latest classical style, oddly modelled on heathen temples, a symmetrical composition with a handsome pediment on which was boldly carved the year 1707. The seven great windows upstairs were balanced by six below, three on each side of a noble doorcase, fit for a king, crowned by a broken pediment (an ornamental device much used in Frome) between which was a flaming urn intimating immortality. The flanking pavilions and gate piers were added in the 19th century when the chapel was also refronted. It had a cupola, described with the 'arched windows' and lack of bells or organ in a letter from Mrs Rowe, the Frome poet, to the Countess of Hertford in 1729. The cupola was provocative and in times of trouble the mob would gather and cry: 'Down with the cupola'. With the original Sheppard's Barton Meeting House, Rook Lane Chapel was said by The *Agreeable Historian* in 1746 to be 'as handsome perhaps as any in England, and there are few more spacious'. It possessed in that year 'two very large beautiful windows beside others', galleries all round, and was supported by the two Doric pillars which are such a feature of the chapel today.

Despite its beautiful building the congregation was not united. In 1744, a section hived off to found a chapel in Starve Acre (Dorset Close) and in 1773, some calvinistic students broke away and founded Zion Congregational Church, meeting in various places until they took over the site of the present chapel in Whittox Lane, then occupied by a Moravian sect. Zion was rebuilt on a generous scale in 1810.

The Baptists and Quakers were also in Frome by the mid-17th century. The first Quakers are mentioned in 1659 and ten years later the Baptists met at Hall House which then belonged to Walter Marchant. Despite their active pastor, Dr John Sharpe, it was not until 1710-11 that they acquired a plot 'in the street leading from Catern Hill to Badcocks' and built Badcox Lane Chapel. Mr Sharpe also had trouble with the mob, which would assemble and cry 'Down with Roundheads'. A powerful man, Sharpe on one occasion put his back to a wall and retorted: 'If any of you think you can down with roundheads, come on'. Although most of the chapels had burial vaults where the fragrance of the dead was not always appreciated by the living, only Badcox Lane (with the exception of the Quakers) acquired a burial ground. This was about 1745 and lay in Wayland's Close behind Catherine Hill, taking some of the pressure off the parish churchyard as the population increased. The chapel became too small for the needs of its members and was rebuilt in 1813, the old Sun Inn being bought and demolished to make way for the new structure.

The Quakers and Presbyterians secured the patronage of John Sheppard, whose family was coming to prominence. John Sheppard, the second son of John the maltster, allowed the Quakers to establish a meeting house and burial ground on his land. John Clare was the first to 'receive the Truth' in Frome. There were six Friends by 1668 and regular meetings of the Society of Friends were being held the following year, when 'the intention of marriage' between Christopher Hillaker and Mary King, both of Frome, was published at one of them. The Quaker meeting house was at the top of South Parade (originally part of Sheppard's Barton). The present building, later occupied by the Red Cross, but now converted to offices, was built in 1821, as appears from records held at the Friends' Meeting House, Street.

Another independent group, at first styled Presbyterians but later Baptists, met in Mr Sheppard's house, the Manor House of St Katherine's Hill, licensed for worship in 1688. In 1707 he sold the land on which Sheppard's Barton Chapel was built, to the congregation. Wellwishers including Sheppard himself (£30), Richard Bull (£75) and Jonathan Whitchurch (£60), subscribed £302 8s. Rev Job David, a later pastor, described it as of a beauty superior to any other chapel in the town. It was much like Rook Lane, the roof upheld by 30 feet Doric columns, and the interior fitted with galleries and a finely carved pulpit and sounding board. The front had eight windows each nine feet high over a span of 42 ft. There were 10 windows in the 'back front' and four in each side. Unlike Rook Lane, it was said to be 'beautiful on all four sides'. *The Agreeable Historian* in 1746 agreed that Sheppard's Barton was superior to Rook Lane 'in the elegance and expense of its fabric, its pews, pillars, and pavement'. This chapel was taken down during Rev Job David's pastorate, and its successor rebuilt in 1850. The Sheppard family remained closely connected with the chapel until well into the 19th century, serving as deacons, adding endowments, and being buried in its vaults. In 1747, John Sheppard gave to the chapel Wine Street House, originally a clothier's house which, judging from the gabled wing at the back, dates back to around 1600. It was let to members of the Sheppard family who improved it with a Georgian front about 1760. The chapel retained the freehold until 1961. The chapel acquired the site of The Old Manse in 1790 and built the house for its minister. The first Sunday School in Frome was started at Sheppard's Barton in 1784.

Leading lights in the movement were Mrs Bunn, of Monmouth House, mother of the Frome worthy, Thomas Bunn, and her daughter, Jane. It was claimed by Sheppard's Barton that Mrs

Bunn previously took pupils in her own house, and had in fact anticipated the national Sunday School movement started by Robert Raikes in Gloucester. The pupils were poor. The Bunns clothed the girls (a boy's school came later) in coloured dresses, from which it became known as the Green School, no doubt to distinguish it from the Blue School.

Numerous were the smaller sects. Their quantity impressed John Wesley. In 1768, he wrote of Frome: 'The people here seem more alive than most... And this is more strange, because in this town only there is such a mixture of men of all opinions, Anabaptists, Quakers, Presbyterians, Arians, Antinonians, Moravians, and what not. If any hold to the truth, in the midst of all these, surely the power must be of God'. The news of the Wesleyan revival came from Bristol via an enthusiastic pedlar in 1746. The first meeting was in Pack Horse Fields, where Christ Church now stands. There was a large crowd but the preacher was pelted with mud, a dead cat and other garbage. Wesley himself preached at Frome for the first time in 1752 and found it 'a dry, barren, uncomfortable place'. The Established Church looked askance at this new sect and Rev Lionel Seaman, Vicar of Frome is credited with having been instrumental in breaking up one of their meetings, at the house of a Mrs Seagram in Whittox Lane, on the ground that she was only licensed for Baptist preachers. The tale is told that when Mrs Seagram and a Mrs Halliday, one of the congregation, were on their way to Taunton to be tried for holding an illegal conventicle, they were ill-treated by a man called Corpe. Mrs Halliday told him: 'Corpe thou shalt stink alive', and sure enough the poor fellow, who was a tallow chandler, later fell into a vat of his own boiling liquid. He was rescued, but broke out into large, stinking ulcers. No one would go near him and he was taken to the Workhouse at Welshmill and apparently locked in a shed by the river. One night the Frome flooded, Corpe was forgotten and drowned. However, this was in 1768, fifteen years after the original incident.

Wesley returned to preach in Frome again and again until 'at length this wilderness too, as it has long appeared to be, begins to blossom and bud as the rose', rather to his surprise for he found it 'exceedingly strange that any considerable good should be done at poor dead quarrelsome Frome'. The people whom he had thought 'rich and increased in goods and needing nothing' began to respond to his teaching. The faithful increased slowly: there were 38 members in 1757 and still only 55 twenty years later. The Methodists met first in Broadway and then moved to a house in Behind Town between the present Wine Street and South Parade, which was converted into a large meeting room with galleries that held 200 people. When Wesley came to preach here in 1767 there was such 'a multitude of all denominations' that they could not be contained in the meeting room. Wesley moved over to Packhorse Fields opposite, where single-stick players, a popular sport in Frome, built him a stage from which to preach. This was Satan serving God, for the Methodists disapproved of single-stick and nicknamed a field in which it took place near the Butts, Hell's Corner. In 1778, Wesley preached in the Market Place to 'a very numerous congregation...they stood as quiet as those at Bristol, a very few excepted, most of whom were, by the courtesy of England, called gentlemen. How much inferior to the keelmen and colliers'. The next year the Methodists bought the site of the present meeting house at Claybatch and, despite the treasurer running off with the funds, successfully completed a large building which seated 420. Wesley preached there the same year. In due time, it was also found to be too small, and the Wesleyan Chapel, which now stands above the busy junction of Bath and Christchurch Streets, was built by James Lester, using the old materials, in 1810-12 for £1,666. Such were the main strands of nonconformity in 18th century Frome. Each chapel had its network of subsidiary meetings through the town, which accounts for the proliferation of chapels. For instance, there were at least seven Baptist chapels at various times. In the 18th century religion in Frome was a seriously enjoyable business of which most partook with relish. Samuel Bowden, doctor and poet, himself a nonconformist and brother of the pastor of Rook Lane, with a good sense of humour summed it up in *The Mechanic Inspir'd,* or the *Methodist's Welcome to Frome,* published in 1754:

Say, brother fanatics, what led you to Frome
Where weavers expound as they sit at the loom;
Where mechanics inspired, the Gospel explain
And weave at a text as well as a chain?
Here tinkers and tailors deep doctrines can handle
By the light of the Spirit—or light of the candle.

Religious disputation throve in a growing population. The serious slump of the 1630s had passed, and the Frome woollen industry entered a period of high prosperity. The old wealth of Frome had been based on the manufacture of a heavy, undyed broadcloth. .Frome now responded to the demand for lighter coloured broadcloths, or medleys, which meant not only the resurgence of the wool trade, but also the introduction of dyeing on a large scale. The town was sufficiently noteworthy by 1721, for a World Atlas to inform its readers that Frome was 'very famous for the manufacture of broad and narrow woollen-cloths, in which it employs thousands of the poor, both old and young, so that girls of 7 or 8 years of age are able to earn half a crown per week in a good time of trade'. The *Agreeable Historian* in 1746 held that the woollen manufacture at Frome had 'thriven here to such a degree that seven waggons have been set out with cloth weekly from this town to Blackwell Hall (the forum where West Country cloth was sold in London). Indeed, all of it was not made in Frome for the clothiers of the neighbouring villages of Elme, Mells, Whatley, Noney, etc., brought their goods hither for carriage to London, and each of these waggons used to hold 140 pieces, which being valued at £14 one with another made the value of the whole to amount in the year to above £700,000 in this quarter of the county'. Cloth-making on such a scale needed vast quantities of good quality cards, good carding being crucial in the making of the yarn. Around 1716 more wire cards were made 'than in all England besides', Yorkshire and the West being supplied from Frome. There were 20 master cardmakers, of whom John Glover, living in 1746, employed 400 men, women, and children.

The opportunity of work, and hope of making money brought people swarming into the town. A housing boom followed. In Frome, contained by its hills and river, expansion was not simple, especially when most wanted to be as near the mills as possible. However, a safety valve was provided by the Manor of St Katherine . This estate, once in the hands of Richard West, who had left his modest mansion house in the Conigre to his wife, was in 1607 sold to John Yerbury, of Atworth in Wiltshire, (a family which originally came from Batcombe and had strong connections with Frome and Laverton). By 1670 it had passed into the hands of Richard Yerbury, who in 1668 was rated for his extensive properties at a total of 5s, a comparatively large sum. Much of the Manor of St Katherine consisted of an area known as the Woadground or close, later corrupted to Oadground. This lay behind the Conigre and West End, sweeping uphill over what were to become Milk and Trinity Streets, across flat land to Vallis Way which already existed. The Oadground took its name from Woad (Isatis tinctoria), a plant from whose leaves was extracted a blue dye, indigo blue, much used in the wool trade, especially for military uniforms. It was also grown in Mells, where a horse mill existed to grind it, the owner being known as Harvey the Woadman. The growing of woad is supposed to have been discontinued after his death, but when Rev Richard Warner visited Frome in 1801 he still found the labouring people 'as deeply tinged as ancient Britons' with the dye. The Oadground was flanked by Vallis Way and the continuation of Whittox Lane, which led down to Low Water and Whatcombe via Dyer's Close Lane. The land between them, on which the area later known as Trinity was to grow, was laid out in enclosed fields, which were to set their pattern on the development. It was not until the 1660s that the demand for building sites began, a demand to which Richard Yerbury responded, by making available on long lease, plots in the flattest and most convenient spot available in the Manor of St Katherine, a recently enclosed field called New Close. It first appears in the Church rates (with the implication that a substantial house had been erected, for the poor were exempt), in 1668. Woad Close is mentioned in 1677 when Richard Stile paid a sixpenny rate on his house there.

As far as the churchwardens were concerned, Oadground and New Close were synonymous. In 1685, there were 47 houses in Oadground and in 1694, 27 were listed at the end of the Town Tithing rate as if they were new. Occasionally the Church rates actually tell us of new houses such as those of Mr Frampton and Solomon Debnam, both in 1693. Although it is only a rough guide because the poorer houses were not counted, there were 60 houses rated in Oadground by 1727, suggesting that the area available must have been fully developed by 1700. New Close, the first field to be built over after 1668, was enclosed between Castle Street, Vallis Way, Naish's Street and Trinity Street. Emboldened by the success of the venture, Yerbury went on to develop his Mill Close on sloping ground which adjoined it to the north-east, an area bounded by Trinity Street, the end of Castle Street (formerly Fountain Lane), Milk Street and Rosemary Lane, a now vanished barton near The Mint. Several fine houses of the period survive, including the old King's Head Inn, now restored, and Mrs Castle's house in Castle Street, its 17th century origins masked by its Georgian brick front. A lease of 1695 from Yerbury to Isaac Pobjoy, tiler, refers to a new house to the north and an empty plot to the south. Pobjoy's plot, 18 ft by 168 ft, has been identified with the site of the Selwood Printing works and shows that Selwood Road was then in the course of development. A plot in Mill Close leased in 1693 to William Coombes, mason, was 74 ft in length and had empty but bespoken plots on each side. John Coward had tenements here in 1694 in a part which came to be called Coward's Batch, where Milk Street, Whittox Lane and Castle Street meet. William Titford had eight houses in Coward's Batch the same year. By that year Yerbury's rates had gone up to 7s 10d. A rent roll of the Manor of St Katherine in 1735 lists 173 tenants, although not all of these were resident. Most were labourers and tradesmen, bakers, cardmakers, carpenters, staymakers, weavers, curriers, and grocers. Most of the rents are a few shillings except for the £5 15s 7d paid by Mrs Usher for 'ye Feild and Ground'. Mrs Usher's lease of a house and garden in New Close survives. It dates from 1725. The garden was not allowed to lie fallow. When the property changed hands in 1750 it also included two cottages, so the expansion continued. Sixty houses sold in Trinity in 1887 had all belonged to the Yerbury estate. An entry in the church rate book for 1705 has a fine ring about it: 'Received of Richard Wiltshire cardmaker for his great new house in Oadground 5d'.

Other landowners were not slow to follow Richard Yerbury's example. That shrewd business woman, Susannah Whitchurch developed the north-west end of Trinity Street and The Mint, an area known as Katherine Close or Street. Many houses were built here around 1718. Plots varied in size from mostly 14 or 18 ft wide and 112 ft in length. A deed of 1733 mentions Middle or Mint Street and Middle Back Side or Barren Alley. John Selwood, who probably built and gave his name to Selwood Farm, the great gabled house which overlooks Spring Gardens, laid out Selwood Close on the north-west side of Naish's Street. The Manor of St Katherine was not the only area of expansion. Early in the 18th century, the Sheppard family built many cottages in Rack Close, soon to become Sheppard's Barton, and developed High Street (literally one of the highest streets in the town) and Wine Street, both of which first appear in the Church rates in 1746. Starve Acre was also built over at this time. There is reference to the New Buildings in Keyford in 1734. The Trinity area has been claimed as the earliest surviving area of planned industrial housing in the country, and its importance generally recognised. Too much must not be made of the planning aspect. It was of the most rudimentary kind, that imposed by the leasing of adjoining plots within an existing framework of hedges and tracks. The rectangular strips of the old field system provided a pattern into which the new roads and dwellings had to fit. The houses, as The Agreeable Historian opined in 1746 were, by and large, 'not indeed very sumptuous nor the streets very spacious'.

The phenomenal expansion of Frome was not lost on the rest of the country. 'Frome-Selwood...is a very great town', declared a World Atlas in 1721, '...reckoned one of the most populous in the West of England.. .This town increases every day in buildings, so that within these 10 years past near 2,000 houses have been built on new foundations'. Daniel Defoe, who knew Frome well, wrote in 1726 that it had 'so prodigiously increased within these 20 or 30 years...that it is now reckoned to have more people in it than the City of Bath'. According to 'Common fame' the population was 10,000. Twenty years later population was estimated at 13,000 'of whom 'tis said one half are newcomers within these 35 years'. John Strachey, who came to Frome himself, was more cautious. He agreed that the population was still increasing, but had looked at the rate books and found that there were 1,031 houses in the whole parish, of which 608 only were in the Town Tithing to which Trinity belonged. He also recorded that the Poor Rate was 'above 800 lb' in 1696, a figure which would fit in with an influx of newcomers who had yet to find homes and jobs.

The figures given by Defoe and the Atlas are, of course, inaccurate. A careful survey carried out for Lord Weymouth in 1785 found that there were 1,684 houses in Frome and 8,185 people. This last figure is confirmed by the 1801 Census which gives the population of Frome as 8,748. But if the travellers exaggerated, they did not belie the truth of the phenomenon. By 1766, Trinity as it existed up to the demolitions of the 1960s was fully established, except that there had been little development in Smith's Orchard, as Gould's Ground was called. Castle Street, then called Long Row, justified its name and continued by Fountain Lane and Coward's Batch to Milk Street and Whittox Lane. Selwood Road existed as two streets, Blunt and Broad, but did not go through to Vallis Way, entering a road called Brandy Lane parallel to it, (now Baker Street). Trinity Row was Grope Lane and York Street, Milking Barton. Naish's Street, named after a local family, has retained its old name. Trinity Street was made up of three sections, Trooper Street (so called from the Trooper Inn), Cross Street, and Nail Street (William Nayle the elder figures in the 1735 rental).

In the demolished area of Trinity were Rosemary Lane, Barren Alley which became Peter Street, The Mint, Kittle Alley, Limerick and Bell Lane. Limerick may get its name from the Irish refugees who were not uncommon in Somerset around 1690, and Bell Lane so-called from the foundry set up there by Lewis Cockey, a member of the famous bell-founding family of Warminster who were also to become prominent townsmen of Frome. Cockey paid a 3d rate for a house in the Oadground in 1685 and 'Cockey ye Brasier" appears in the 1735 St Katherine's rental. A deed of 1773 makes mention of Lewis Cockey's premises, called the Bell House. It is possible that trade tokens were made here and that this gave rise to that pleasant street name, The Mint.

In that part of Trinity developed by the Whitchurch family: The Mint, levelled in the 1960s. (FM)

ABOVE LEFT: Butchers' shop at the Badcox entrance of Castle Street, demolished in 1904. RIGHT: Starve Acre, re-named Union Street in the 19th century, which has now vanished under Dorset Close. BELOW: The upper end of Trinity Street in 1904, showing the Bell Inn on the left. (FM)

ABOVE LEFT: Lost cottages. These were opposite Milk Street School. The house with labels over the windows was an inn known as Dr Andrews'. RIGHT: Bell Lane in 1962, giving a glimpse of the Selwood Printing Works. (FM) BELOW LEFT: The hilly part of Castle Street, once known as Fountain Lane, with characteristic houses, and RIGHT: another group of houses which went in the clearances of the early '60s: Peter Street.

ABOVE LEFT: Demolition in progress in the Trinity area. RIGHT: The first stage of the re-development nears completion: the last house to go. BELOW: Saved for posterity: substantial houses in Vallis Way. One is dated 1697, contemporary with the buildings in the Trinity area.

LEFT: Lord of the Manor: John, Earl of Cork and Orrery. (GHB) RIGHT: The Angel Inn, King Street: mentioned in 1668. (FM) BELOW: Squire Champneys' headquarters: the garden front of Orchardleigh House in 1832.(AD)

The Changing Years

Despite the finery of its merchant princes, Frome was a rough, tough place in the early 18th century, much given to lawlessness and riot. By 1721, it was already well-known for brewing.a strong, stale beer which may have contributed to the disturbances. This was said to be preferred by the gentry to the finest French wines or Port, and certainly Lord Orrery and his Frome friends were much given to partaking of 'October', as it was called, at their convivial get-togethers in the George Kitchen and at Hall House. October was kept in large quantities and to a great age. At a later date Rev John Nightingale found at the Bell 'a cask which is shewn as a curiosity to strangers. It will contain not less than six hundred puncheons' (a puncheon was 72 gallons). The 1774 plan of Frome shows more than 40 pubs and alehouses, a conservative estimate. Of these, the Bell in Behind Town is the earliest to be mentioned by name, about 1580. It had closed by 1832. The Angel in King Street appears in the rental of Lord Stourton's property in 1668; at the same time there was another Angel in Church Slope. The George is first named in 1650 when Sir John Horner and Mr Bampfylde, the Squire of Hardington, met there. The Swan at Badcox is listed in the Church Rate in 1686. A deed of 1710 refers to the Black Boy in Wallbridge, another in 1731 to the Wheatsheaves in Cock Street (Eagle Lane). Drunkenness was commonplace.

Apart from drinking, cock-fighting, boxing, bull and bear-baiting were popular (there was a bear pit at Egford Hill). Single-stick combats were much enjoyed, special stages being set up in Badcox and Packhorse Fields. Fighting was frequent and punished by a spell in the pillory or a whipping through the town. Much to the dismay of the Vestry, the prosperity of Frome brought in 'great numbers of vagrants and other loose, idle and disorderly persons (who) do frequently resortte and infest this parish and are harboured and entertained by diverse evil minded persons who keepe lodgings for them and sell beer, etc., strong waters and other liquors without licences to the great detriment and danger of the inhabitants in their persons and goods...'. In 1730, the Vestry determined to put a stop to this, but had a new problem the following year, when Frome was found to be unsafe at night, people being tripped up and robbed by men with iron crooks on long poles. The ordinances of the Vestry were handed down by the bellman, who went about in his 'grete cote' announcing each item of news. Rev Lionel Seaman, who became Lord of the Manor of Frome in 1738 and Vicar four years later, was a civilised man and tried to put a stop to bull-baiting and raffling in pubs. This made him extremely unpopular in some quarters and he received anonymous letters threatening his life. One contained his epitaph:

You that pass by pray stop and see this grave,   Pity'd by none for his untimely fall.
Here lyes the body of a rogue and knave   Froom would not have been back again'tis true
Who draw'd upon himself the hate of all;   For all the gold and silver in Peru.

There was trouble in Frome in 1726 when the weavers rioted and made common cause with those of Wiltshire. Mrs Rowe wrote to Lady Hertford 'very sedately' against a background of 'the noise of a mob of thousands of clothiers workmen, and the grenadiers firing power to fright them, but to no purpose'. Her only fear was that she would be unable to get to the post-house. By the end of the year all was quiet, with a troop of Dragoons stationed in the town and some of the ringleaders sent to Ilchester jail. Squire Champneys was particularly commended for his zeal and diligence in hunting them down.

Much building went on in Frome in the decades after 1740. English cloth, after a steep decline in demand in the late 1730s, was so much sought after that, as Lady Hertford wrote to her son, Lord Beauchamp in August 1743, 'they cannot make it fast enough to satisfy the call for it; and they cannot at this time in Wiltshire, Somersetshire, and all the western counties get labourers to bring in their harvest because all the poor people are employed by the clothiers...'. She ascribed this prosperity to the Turks, who would deal with no one else. An attempt seems to have been made to improve communications with London and to provide better accommodation for visitors. In 1739, a new inn was built north of Frome Bridge to serve as the London coach office (it had closed by 1800). The Champneys Arms, as it was called after the owner of the site, is now 2, North Parade and of particular interest as we have the exact specifications laid down for the building. It was to be 'a good substantial well timbered house', 38 ft in the front and 16 ft in breadth, with three floors and three rooms to a floor each more than 8 ft in height. The tenant, William Baily, 'joyner' was to 'pargett and ceil all the roomes of the dwelling house with lime and haire'. Even the garrets were to be well-lighted and glazed with crown glass. There was to be a brewhouse, of course, and (piece de resistance) a tennis or ball court with a 'tower', presumably the wall at the end, 45 ft high of 'good ashlar freestone'. The tennis court must have been a talking point in Frome, as the property is always referred to in the Church rates and Land Tax assessments by that name. A rival establishment was the Waggon and Horses in Gentle Street, from whose back premises in Clavey's Barton, which skirted the old tithe barn and came out into Christchurch Street East to the east of the present Blindhouse Lane, 'the old standing constant Froome flying waggon' set out for London each Monday at one o'clock. It was supposed to arrive on Wednesday at noon at the King's Arms in Holborn. The fare was £1 7s 0d. Joseph Clavey, the enterprising proprietor, was churchwarden in 1744.

The greatest builder, although it was not given to him to achieve all he hoped, was the new and vigorous vicar, Dr Lionel Seaman, who as Lord of the Manor and Vicar combined the resources of Church and State. An active shepherd of his flock, he did not care to live at the remote and now dilapidated Manor House at Vallis, but in the town centre. The old vicarage stood close to its present site. Samuel Bowden implies that it was an ancient building, like many in Frome much decayed ('where late an old monastic structure stood, in ruins clad...'). Dr Seaman resolved to pull it down altogether. This was done and the Vicar laid the foundation stone of the new building on 29 May, 1744. This had a disastrous effect on the adjoining free school and library, which the Vestry went to view and found 'the same in so ruinous condition that it must inevitably fall on the removal of the Vicaridge walls'. At their meeting on 10 June, 1744, the Vestry ordered the building to be taken down and the materials preserved. At the same time it was resolved to rebuild the church tower and steeple, which was in such a poor state of repair that the bells could not be rung, and there were rumours that the steeple had collapsed. The Vestry resolved to ascertain the view of John Wood the elder, the famous Bath architect, but unfortunately no record of his opinion remains. In the end, a local builder, Henry Fisher, carried out repairs.

In February, 1749, the new vicarage, classical in style and in the height of fashion, was completed and duly honoured by Samuel Bowden in a lively poem:

> A finish'd fabric now salutes the day,
> With pleasing pomp magnificently gay,
> Where yawning arches nodded all around,
> The fair creation rises from the ground;
> In graceful elegance attracts the sight,
> Smiles o'er the ruins, and dispels the night.

Dr Seaman's cottage *orne* was altered by Charles Phillot after he became Vicar in 1813 and substantially rebuilt by Rev W. J. E. Bennett (1852-1886), who added a chapel. The new free, or grammar school, was built by Henry Spencer for £106 and seems to have been completed by 1746, when the Vestry ordered that desks for the school and shelves for the library were to be provided out of deal boards used for a scaffold for the steeple. This too, reflected Dr Seaman's taste, classical in inspiration, a high round-arched doorway with a keystone being flanked by similar windows. In front was a court with a wall and handsome gate piers. The one room proving inadequate, the court was filled in to make an ante-room in 1798. As usual Dr Bowden was on hand to greet the new arrival in verse, comparing it with the grander vicarage:

> Close by the pile, where stood the ancient hall
> A new gymnasium rears its humbler wall,
> Religion thus, with learning in her eye,
> Together rise—and shall together die.

Under the direction of Rev Peter Mayson, who served as curate at St John's from 1765 to 1787, the grammar school had a high reputation and 'many respectable persons' were educated there. These included Lord Dungarvan, later 7th Earl of Cork and Orrery, and Samuel Reddish (1735-1785) son of a Frome tradesman who, despite his stiff and heavy form, rigid face, and monotonous voice, became a well-known London actor remembered for the violence of his style. It may be that Sir Charles Wilkins, born in Frome in 1749, who joined the East India Company, became the first to acquire a thorough grasp of sanskrit, and a Fellow of the Royal Society was at this school, but we cannot be certain. There was no residence for the teacher and when Rev John Pococke became schoolmaster in 1795 he lived opposite at Westbrook House, using two large chambers at the back as schoolrooms. Pococke, described by Thomas Bunn as the most conceited man he ever knew, took private pupils and derived a large income from the school. When he died in 1804 his effects were sold and the school property with them. Although Rev W. M. H. Williams was appointed master of the grammar school in 1819 and the Crown grant was continued until 1865, the building in Vicarage Street was abandoned and the school became a private one held in various big houses, although Mr Williams, in 1836, agreed to take free,children of those legally entitled to send them 'when his obligations in this respect shall be ascertained'. Rev W.J.E. Bennett pulled down the grammar school in the 1850s, and, fashion having come full circle, erected on the site St John's Hall (then an infants' school), in a Gothic style more to his taste.

In other parts of Frome large classical houses were erected for mill owners and others. The Aliens, wealthy dyers in Pilly (Willow) Vale built Willow Vale House before 1739. Timothy Lacey, a mercer, erected North Hill House in a commanding position overlooking the town, after his marriage to Eleanor Sheppard in 1763 (it has since been spoilt and made somewhat top heavy by an additional storey), and about the same time George Whitchurch, an attorney, put up Catherine Hill House with its splendid rooms and doorway enhanced by Doric columns and a frieze. This house which, apart from its intrinsic merit, has vaulted cellars and a mediaeval drain, fell into a bad state of repair but was well restored from 1980. Miss Mary Jesser built the original Argyll House (so-called from a Duchess of Argyll who occupied it in 1855) in Gentle Street in 1766. The Jessers, who had a dyehouse at Welshmill, were discerning collectors of pictures, plate and china They had their portraits painted by the fashionable Bath artist, William Hoare, and were on terms of friendship with the cultured Earl of Orrery at Marston. Mary Jesser whose family had a predilection for the Chinese taste which had become the rage about 1755, installed a 'Chinese Chippendale' staircase of fine workmanship at Argyll House, which still remains. Another development in Gentle Street shortly before this date was the creation of Gentle Street House, now The Chantry and The Hermitage. This was the work of the third James Wickham (1721-1791), a solicitor, who in 1744 started a diary, which was kept up by succeeding generations at least until 1850, but has disappeared. We would give a good deal to peruse those volumes now. In 1761, he acquired a lease of these properties from Lord Weymouth, sometimes erroneously said to be the Thynne town house, and set about creating a mansion worthy of his family. He replaced the old mullions with sash windows and made other interior improvements. He leased ruinous cottages in Twattle Alley, which ran along the top of the churchyard, and, pulling them down, created a large terraced garden. Not content with this, he bought cottages opposite (where Knoll House now stands), demolished them and made a fine lawn, across which he looked to Rook Lane ChapeL This conversion of an old building was unusual. It remained the home of the Wickhams until they bought North Hill House shortly before 1800. The 'priest's hole', or oratory, in The Chantry is probably in reality a dry larder.

Dr Seaman, who became Archdeacon of Taunton in 1753, threw off the burden of secular authority by selling the Manor of Frome to John, Earl of Cork and Orrery in 1751.The Boyle family, to which the earl belonged, had bought the Manor of Marston Bigot in 1641, but had rarely been resident until John Boyle succeeded to the Orrery title in 1731 (he became Earl of Cork in succession to a cousin in 1753). Lord Cork took a great interest in Frome and, although secretly proud of his lineage and title, ostensibly treated the Frome clothiers as equals, much to their satisfaction. One of his first actions was to rebuild the George Hotel, the accounts speaking of alabaster for the great room and freestone chimney pieces. He was much taken with Vallis Manor—'a most delightful situation and vast command'—where he spent time cutting ivy and pruning trees. As befitted the author of a life of Dean Swift and the translator of the letters of Pliny the younger, he had 'a little closet of books within' and was given to stretching his legs in 'a large antique room', probably the Great Hall. Vallis was already a farm and any plans Lord Cork may have had to refurbish it were cut short by his premature death in 1762. A devotee of literature in a dilettante fashion, he found the vicinity somewhat lacking in kindred spirits. He knew Mrs Elizabeth Rowe, but she died in 1737, after which he had to make do with the ubiquitous Dr Samuel Bowden, who dedicated several poems to him and members of his family. On one occasion Dr Bowden appeared at Marston and saluted Lord Orrery (as he then was) in the following manner:

Fair be the morn, spotless the azure sky,
When Bowdens thus attends his Orrery.

'That I might not be behind hand with the Doctor,' recorded Orrery, 'I endeavoured to recover my skill at versification and after a short pause replied:

Sacred Physician All that's bright must follow,
When I'm thus honour'd by the Froome Apollo.'

A marvellously vivid glimpse of a polite but warm exchange between two friends near Frome in the Spring of 1745. Cork was the first of his family to be buried in St John's, apparently without incident, although when his son Hamilton, the sixth earl, was laid to rest two years later, the churchwardens spent 2s to 'keep off the mob'. The Earls of Cork and Orrery remained Lords of the Manor and owners of much of Frome until 1905, the double Irish title becoming a natural part of the Somerset scene.

Serious unrest occurred in Frome in 1757 because of the high price of food. The colliers from the coalmines around Radstock, often a potent factor in Frome affairs, were at the heart of it. In April, 200 of them broke into a mealman's house and had to be suppressed by a party of soldiers from Bruton. In May, a mob of women upset the market in trying to get the price of potatoes reduced by half. More serious trouble came at the end of May, on which a correspondent of the *London Chronicle* reported: 'I had a very disagreeable sight of the two men that were killed and four wounded in a riot of the colliers that morning (27 May) aside of Frome, where in a quarter of an hours time, they entirely pulled down and destroyed a flour mill and were marching to do the same to another...but met with so warm a reception from eight persons only, well armed with a blunderbuss, guns and pistols' that 400 or 500 were entirely routed leaving two dead. Three of the wounded also died. 'One man had 16 balls through the brim of his hat and received no hurt... The valiant miller (of the second mill) has a blunderbuss which, he told me with some pleasure, would carry 18 balls complete at one charge'. The women again took the law into their own hands in 1766 when they seized a load of flour and divided it among the poor.

The life of a young Frome gentlewoman at the end of the 18th century is reflected in a diary kept by Miss Susan Bunn in 1782 and 1783. She was a sister of Thomas Bunn and died young in 1784. Most of her time was spent making and receiving visits from people of similar standing. Much time in warm weather was spent promenading, the fashionable place being the high pavement in Wallbridge, known as the Coalash Walk or Wallbridge Terrace, then giving wide views over the countryside so that Miss Bunn 'much enjoyed the agreeable scene' around her. Vallis Vale was considered extremely romantic and was .the venue for musical parties and picnics:

> There winds a vale so smooth and green,
> So soft and lovely is the scene,
> That Nature's lover has not smiled,
> On scenes more beautifully wild.

Presumably the lower classes who assembled there in 'large and numerous groups' during the summer had to be avoided. There were weddings, an elopement where it could not be decided which of three young men was the culprit, a sight of Mr Walter Sheppard's pretty new phaeton, and special highlights such as a visit to Rev Richard Graves, the author, at Widcombe, or a reception at Mells Park. On one occasion Miss Bunn was 'very unwell...a touch of the present fashionable complaint which half the Town are confined with'. On 20 May, 1782, Frome was 'very gay' with a large bonfire and general illuminations to celebrate the capture by Admiral Rodney of 'six capital men of war belonging to the French'. In 1800, Mr Shatford's company of players were reported in Frome. They performed more than 50 plays, one 'for the benefit of the poor'.

According to Rev John Collinson's *History of Somerset,* published in 1791, Frome contained 38 streets, 13 lanes and 12 courts or bartons. 'Most of the streets are narrow and irregular, without paving, except some narrow foot-ways on one side of rough stone, of which the houses are chiefly constructed'. He adds ominously that it had been famous for woollen cloth 'which of late (it is said) has been rather declining than increasing'. However, 160,000 yards of cloth from 1450 packs of wool each weighing 240 lbs were still produced each year. Collinson's strictures on Frome roads were echoed by Dr Maton, who came on a tour in search of scenery and antiquities between 1794 and 1796. Thomas Bunn at a later date recalled that 'The town was one of the worst, if not the very worst in the county of Somerset. The thoroughfares mere lanes, so narrow that carriages could not pass each other without ascending the footways'. There had been some improvements. The Turnpike system had been introduced in 1663 under which local trustees undertook responsibility for making decent roads in return for tolls from the travelling public. Taunton had been the first town in Somerset to ask for an Act, when it was joked that those ways already existing might as well be turned into canals as roads. As far as Frome was concerned, there was an Act for the improvement of Bonnyleigh Hill in 1752, followed by one in 1757 'for repairing and widening several roads leading to, through, and from the Town of Frome'. This affected the roads from the Bell Inn (Fairlawn House) in Behind Town through Egford and Whatley to Tattle House (Tadhill) near Leigh-on-Mendip, from Egford Bridge to Mells, those near the Swan Inn, 'from Shepherds Steps (sic) leading into a ground called Rack Close' to Murtry Bridge, Wallbridge to Chapmanslade, from 'the Ship Alehouse' to Lipeat in Kilmersdon, Lock's Hill, then known as Lock's Lane, and Water Lane (not the modern lane of that name but Rossiter's Hill) from an alehouse called the Castle and Arch, presumably a predecessor of the Beehive. This Act improved communications but left the centre of the town untouched. A supplementary Act of 1797 allowed the trustees to undertake street lighting and paving. They were also empowered to make a new road from Frome Bridge to the Turnpike road to Beckington over North Hill, because that in existence was 'very narrow and incommodious for travellers and carriages'. The result was the creation of North Parade. The improvements were to be continued with the construction of Bath Street in the next century.

Of the houses, they may have been rough, not indicating 'the wealth that is usually attendant on commerce' and 'very different from the elegant dwellings that are to be found in the Yorkshire manufacturing towns' as Sir Frederick Eden pointed out in his *Report on the State of the Poor* in 1797, but they were generally roomy, well-built and covered with slate or tile. Usually, there was only one family per house. Nor were 'elegant dwellings lacking'. West Lodge in Christchurch Street West, a copy, except for some refinements of detail, of Argyll House, was completed in 1780. It was the last of the old style classical houses. Its first occupant was a surgeon called Houston and it remains a doctor's house today. Leaders of taste were now adopting the chaste and dignified style made popular by Robert Adam. An excellent example is the building in Welshmill Road now divided and known as Mendip House and Welshmill House. This was built about 1790 by Robert Meares, a dyer, who in his spare time invented 'a swivel and socket for the perches of four-wheeled carriages' which prevented them being overturned: and made them run more easily. Even grander was Fromefield House, erected in 1797 by George Sheppard on his marriage. Wallbridge House has this same Adamesque flavour. Garston House, built the same year as Fromefield House, represents the beginning of the reaction against Adam. It is a solid business-like house with paired windows and substantial portico. Garston Lodge (Toops) and Keyford House, built after 1799 but before 1813, display the ultimate reaction of the Gothic revival. Garston House was the home of John Douglas Middleton, a banker, and carrier between Frome and London. In 1808, his house and business were insured for the large sum of £3,400.

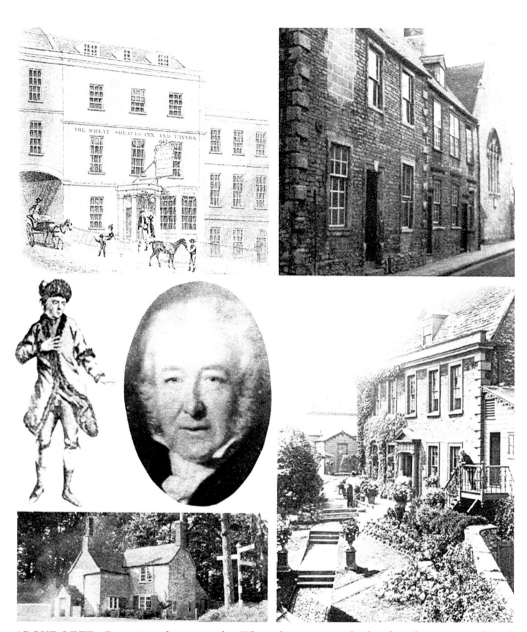

ABOVE LEFT: Georgian elegance: the Wheatsheaves as rebuilt after the cutting of Bath Street. From a trade card. (SAS) RIGHT: On the site of the old Grammar School: St John's Hall and the Georgian houses which were flattened to make way for the present car park. CENTRE LEFT: Samuel Reddish, the Frome born actor, in his role as Posthumus. (BC) RIGHT: James Anthony Wickham, of North Hill House, head of an influential Frome family. (JWL) BELOW LEFT: Turnpike cottage at Styles Hill, now demolished; (FM) and RIGHT: Catherine Hill House, home of George Whitchurch, attorney. (FM)

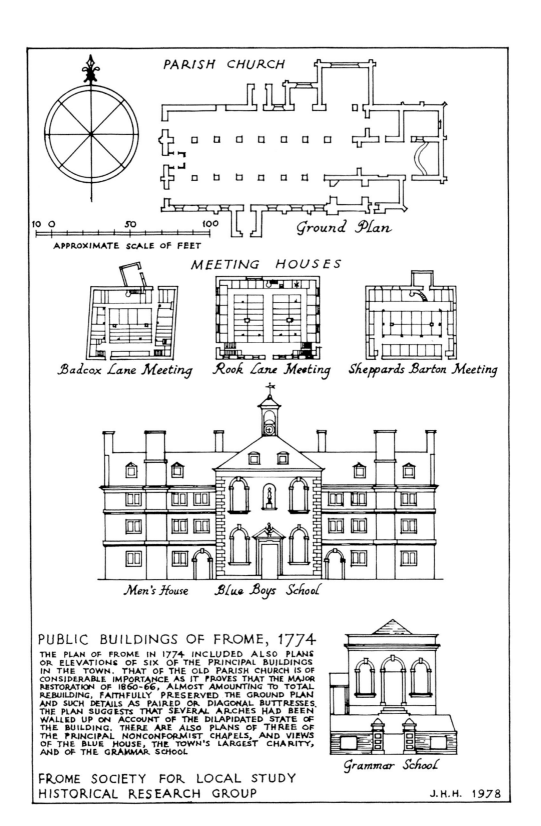

PARISH CHURCH

APPROXIMATE SCALE OF FEET

Ground Plan

MEETING HOUSES

Badcox Lane Meeting   *Rook Lane Meeting*   *Sheppards Barton Meeting*

Men's House   *Blue Boys School*

PUBLIC BUILDINGS OF FROME, 1774

THE PLAN OF FROME IN 1774 INCLUDED ALSO PLANS
OR ELEVATIONS OF SIX OF THE PRINCIPAL BUILDINGS
IN THE TOWN. THAT OF THE OLD PARISH CHURCH IS OF
CONSIDERABLE IMPORTANCE AS IT PROVES THAT THE MAJOR
RESTORATION OF 1860-66, ALMOST AMOUNTING TO TOTAL
REBUILDING, FAITHFULLY PRESERVED THE GROUND PLAN
AND SUCH DETAILS AS PAIRED OR DIAGONAL BUTTRESSES.
THE PLAN SUGGESTS THAT SEVERAL ARCHES HAD BEEN
WALLED UP ON ACCOUNT OF THE DILAPIDATED STATE OF
THE BUILDING. THERE ARE ALSO PLANS OF THREE OF
THE PRINCIPAL NONCONFORMIST CHAPELS, AND VIEWS
OF THE BLUE HOUSE, THE TOWN'S LARGEST CHARITY,
AND OF THE GRAMMAR SCHOOL

Grammar School

FROME SOCIETY FOR LOCAL STUDY
HISTORICAL RESEARCH GROUP

J.H.H. 1978

ABOVE LEFT: Mendip and Welshmill Houses, built in the Adam style. (FM) RIGHT: Monmouth House—it is from here that Thomas Bunn planned the improvement of Frome. (CB) CENTRE LEFT: Byrlton House has been recently repaired and it now makes a fine sight in Selwood Road. RIGHT: Garston House, where banker and carrier John Douglas Middleton lived. Its solid classical dignity makes a telling contrast with BELOW LEFT: Garston Lodge, which was altered in the Gothic revival style popular in 1800. (T) RIGHT: Trade card of Henry Buckle of the George Inn, dated mid- 18th century.

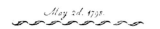

May 2d. 1798.

FROME
Military Affociation.

At a Meeting of the Houfeholders of this Town, for the purpofe of forming a *Military Affociation*, for the Defence of the faid Town and Neighbourhood.

The Rev. W. IRELAND in the Chair.

The following Refolutions were propofed and unanimoufly agreed to : viz.

THAT a Corps of *Volunteer Infantry*, compofed of Houfeholders and fuch other Perfons as fhall be recommended by two Houfeholders, be immediately raifed, for the purpofe of local Defence and the Prefervation of the internal Tranquility of the faid Town.

THAT a Corps of *Volunteer Cavalry* be raifed, for the Defence of the Town and Neighbourhood.

THAT the Rev. W. IRELAND, Mr. WICKHAM, Mr. W. SHEPPARD, Mr. BUNN, Mr. GEORGE, Mr. MIDDLETON, Mr. MAPP, Mr. YEOMAN, Mr. MEARES, Mr. CARTER, Mr. LACEY, Mr. J. BAILEY, Rev. J. POCOCK, Mr. HENRY SHEPPARD, Mr. WHITE, Mr. G. SHEPPARD, Mr. J. WAYLAND, Mr. OLIVE, Mr. KINGDON, Mr. JAMES FORD, Mr. GEORGE CLEMENT, and Mr. JAMES CLEMENT be a Committee, who are hereby empowered to make fuch Rules and Orders, to regulate and direct the Affociation, as they fhall from time to time judge to be requifite. Five members of fuch Committee to be competent for fuch Purpofe.

THAT fuch Uniform as fhall be fixed on by the Committee fhall be provided by each Member at his own expence.

THAT the Officers fhall be recommended by the Corps at large to the Lord Lieutenant, who fhall requeft Commiffions from his Majefty ; and that the Committee be empowered to refufe the admiffion of any Individual to this Affociation, who fhall appear to them unfit to be a Member of the fame.

THAT the Officers and Privates do ferve without pay or other emolument.

THAT Government be folicited to furnifh Arms ; together with a fufficient number of Drill Serjeants, Drummers and Fifers.

THAT the Officers and Privates do perfect themfelves individually, as foon as poffible, in the Exercife, and that they do attend two Hours, *twice* at leaft in every week, to go through the Evolutions together ; and that *once* in every Month at leaft, they attend a General Field Day.

THAT the faid Corps fhall be Commanded by its own Officers, and the Infantry not fubject to be called out of the Town and Parifh of FROME, but the Cavalry to extend their Protection as far as any next adjoining Town not exceeding *twenty* miles.

THAT in cafe of abfence from duty, without a fufficient caufe, allowed by the Commanding Officer, an Officer fhall forfeit *Five Shillings*, and a Private *Two Shillings*.

THAT if the number of Cavalry fhall not, in the courfe of a Month from the date of thefe Refolutions, amount to Sixty, and of Infantry to One Hundred, the deficiency may be fupplied by Men properly recommended by two Houfeholders, which any Perfon fhall be at liberty to fend, and to pay for their uniform and fervice.

THAT a fubfcription be opened, and that it be particularly defired from fuch Perfons who cannot give their Perfonal Attendance, the better to carry thefe Refolutions into effect, under the direction of the Committee.

THAT thefe Refolutions be fairly copied into a Book, and figned by every Member of this Affociation, both as a teftimony of his approbation and as a pledge of his due obfervance of the fame ; and that a printed Copy be delivered to each Member.

THAT thefe Refolutions be tranfmitted to the Lord Lieutenant of this County for his Majefty's gracious Approbation.

> WILLIAM IRELAND, Chairman

The Chairman having left the Chair, Refolved unanimoufly, That the thanks of this Meeting be given to him, for his very proper Conduct.

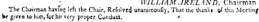

ABOVE LEFT: Contemporary account of the first meeting of the Military Association. BELOW: Sheppards' Factory at Spring Gardens falling into ruin cl900. (FM) ABOVE RIGHT: Edmund, seventh Earl of Cork and Orrery, was buried by the Volunteers. A miniature by Cosway, and BELOW: Edmund, the eighth Earl, builder of the Assembly Rooms, a portrait by Hoppner. (GHB)

Rich and Poor

The wars with France affected Frome in a variety of ways. By 1797, 800 Frome men had entered the army, which meant an increase in the poor rate as their families were chargeable. Frome showed its patriotism by subscribing £473 over and above normal taxes as a contribution to the defence of the country. Messrs Sheppard gave £100 and Mr Middleton, the carrier, another £100. In 1798, at a meeting at the George Inn presided over rather surprisingly by the vicar, Rev William Ireland, a military association of cavalry and infantry, to be known as the Frome Selwood Volunteers, was formed as a local defence force. Thomas Champneys, who had recently come to live at Orchardleigh, and was to be High Sheriff of Somerset in 1800, became colonel. The duties of the Volunteers were largely ceremonial. When the seventh Earl of Cork died in 1798 at Bath, they escorted the coffin into the town, proceeding to St John's 'in slow and decorous movement suitable to the solemnity of the occasion'. They also buried one of their volunteers who died of consumption, with full military honours. They frequented the George and the Crown and became something of a joke. When there was trouble among the colliers and it was proposed to call them out (the colliers had put up a gallows on which they threatened to hang the masters), the officers were advised, only partly in jest, not to give the volunteers notice as 'half of them will not come if they think there is any danger'. As for Colonel Champneys, his debts and love of litigation were to provide Frome with delicious gossip and scandal for nearly 40 years. He did, however, know how to set an example: at a splendid masquerade which he gave at Orchardleigh House in 1801, supper was served in 'richest profusion', but because of the severity of 'existing circumstances' the use of bread was prohibited.

Before the war much kerseymere (a coarse woolled cloth) had been exported to France. This market was now lost, but more than compensated for by the demand for a claret dyed cloth for military uniforms. This was made by Sheppards, which under the direction of William Sheppard (1762-1804), of Styles Hill, and his brother, George (1773-1855), of Fromefield House, expanded dramatically during these years, and fought off the challenge of the Yorkshire woollen and worsted industry. This was not easy, as Yorkshire was becoming increasingly efficient through the adoption of the factory system, spinning jenny, shearing frame and gig mill for dressing cloth. Spinning jennies were burnt, and riots occurred in Frome as early as 1781. Matters were so bad that Samuel Jesser asked that the 4th Regiment of Dragoons at Salisbury should be sent to restore order. Later the factory system and the gig mill were both resisted, even though Sheppard offered to guarantee wages in return for acceptance of the gig mill. This created problems for the Sheppards, as their customers preferred machine finished cloth, so they were reduced to sending it 80 miles into Gloucestershire to be finished. In 1803, weaving was still a cottage industry in Frome. That year saw the attempt to introduce the gig mill in the Wiltshire cloth towns and serious riots, the suppression of which was followed by the repeal of the old legislation, which had tied the hands of the clothiers. The introduction of machinery, and with it the factory system, followed. The first factory was built in Frome by Samuel Humphries at the top of South Parade in 1807. It was later taken over by the firm of

Rawlings, who made cards and belting for driving machines. The factory still exists and may incorporate parts of the original building; it has recently been converted for housing.

Messrs Sheppards started a mill at Spring Gardens with which their name became chiefly associated about 1788. There seems to be no documentary support for the story that the area was formerly called Wind Ash. It had been known as Oldfield since the 13th century. George Sheppard is said to have coined the name Spring Gardens, but it first appears in 1776. The Sheppards acquired Rodden Flour Mill, where they had a factory until the 1860s, in 1793, and by 1800 had extensive works in Pilly Vale. The great complex of factories in Spring Gardens was built in 1809, 1815, and 1824, while in 1811 Sheppards acquired Frome's first steam engine. It was made by Boulton and Watt. In 1805, they were the only firm in Frome making fine cloth and cassimeres (a particularly fine woollen cloth) entirely from Spanish and German wool. The Emperor Alexander of Russia wore Sheppard's superior cloth. It was said that the defeat of Napoleon in 1815 was also one for Sheppards as it ended the war, and so the demand for cloth for uniforms. However, Sheppards knew better and a whole sheep was roasted in celebration. By 1833, they employed 2,000 hands and ran four steam engines. It is interesting that 1500 of these hands were still working in their own homes. The steam engines ended dependence on water power. Sometimes in summer there was just not enough, and the children would be sent out to play as no work was available. The plight of the minor mills higher up the stream is neatly summed up in the couplet: 'Slades and Nappers are shut down, there's no water up to town'. From time to time employees living near the factory were summoned to work at midnight on Sunday, so that use could be made of the water which had gathered during the day. Edward Sheppard considered the factory system more honest, for the further away from the factory the weaving was done the worse it was. Nevertheless, the factory was lit by bright green or red candles to guard against theft.

A strict benevolence characterised the Sheppards as employers. They encouraged Sunday schools, and when Frome possessed only a single bookshop 'the chief stock of which consisted of a circulating library of dirty novels', started a lending library of improving books. In 1833, they built a school opposite Fromefield House for the children of their estate workers and servants, while at the Spring Gardens Factory the children were also taught to read and to listen to the New Testament. All the workpeople received five shillings at Christmas and when the top factory at Spring Gardens was opened in 1824 each employee received a pound (women five shillings). Many children worked at the factory and George Sheppard would go down at six in the morning to see them arrive. If the boys did not go up the steps sharply enough he hurried them up with his stick. Another view of Sheppards was recounted to Anthony Pearman in 1890 by 'Old Man Barter', who had worked at Spring Gardens 60 years before. He said conditions were unbelievably harsh, and that when the mill was busy, they often did not leave it from Monday morning until Saturday night. They slept for six hours from midnight huddled up on piles of woolpacks, to be woken in the morning by the foreman's whip. On moonlit nights some of that time was taken up outside, stealing apples or turnips to fill their empty stomachs. As for the Bibles, they were not much good according to Barter, as not one in 20 could read. When not attending to business, George Sheppard was renowned for his princely hospitality at Fromefield House. His grocery bill was said to be larger than that of the Earl of Cork at Marston House. Thomas Bunn wrote amusingly of the family in 1844: 'The Sheppards were short and many of them plain a few generations back but they marry so many beautiful ladies that they will soon become tall and handsome'.

Visiting Frome in 1801, Rev Richard Warner found 'an agreeable appearance of bustle and business...everything indicates the presence of manufacturers and trade'. No wonder. Apart from the many clothiers, there were the dyers. The Olive family had 19 dyeing vats and 11 furnaces in Pilly (Willow) Vale and Justice Lane. Two of their round drying stoves built before 1813 remain. Edmund Crabb Olive (1803-1877) added to the old Allen house in Willow Vale and is said to have used mahogany from the barrels in which his dyes came from America. Messrs Meares, a family which carried on a dyeing business at Wallbridge Mills for three generations until 1834, had 12 vats and six furnaces. Mr Button had a dyehouse at Welshmill, while Jeffries at Spring Gardens employed 14 men and had three vats. There were many smaller dyers and a host of minor clothiers, of whom one of the chief was Brittains in Vallis Way, who took Henry Houston into partnership in 1829. Under this name the firm continued on the site until the Second World War. They made a cassimere of the finest fabric, which was bought for the harem of the Sultan of Turkey at Constantinople. Other industries established in Frome about this time were silk throwing at Merchant's Barton, and a small printing firm set up by Abraham Crocker, Master of the Blue School, and his sons. Edward Cockey, whose family had been braziers in the town since 1685, had premises in the Upper Market Place in 1808, but later moved over to ironfounding and to Palmer Street. An ambitious project for the promotion of commerce, which might have benefitted Frome greatly, was the Dorset and Somerset Canal, intended to be cut between Bristol and Poole. It was to have touched both Frome and Wincanton. One of the committee meetings was held at the George Inn, Frome, in 1794 and the canal authorised by Act of Parliament in 1796. Much work was actually done before money ran out in 1803 and the scheme was abandoned. Its route can still be seen between Murtry Bridge and Whatcombe Farm, partly as an empty bed and partly as a walled embankment under Selwood Farm, known in Frome as 'the Roman Wall'. One of the most moving relics of the ill-fated undertaking is the spacious aqueduct of finely cut ashlar on the Mells River below Murtry Bridge. This beautiful structure, which would not be out of place in a landscaped Palladian park, looks odd amid the rampant vegetation.

The Napoleonic Wars did not prevent men looking confidently to the future, and in 1796, Richard Stevens, a leather currier and native of Frome, left £12,000 to found an asylum for poor girls, and a further £7,000 to build and endow a hospital for old men 'past their labour'. The trustees lost no time in buying land at Keyford and the foundation stone of 'Keyford Home', as it was often called, was laid on 22 March, 1798. The building, which housed both the hospital and the asylum under one roof, was completed by 1803 at a cost of £6,439 18s. Ten girls were admitted in 1804, the number increased later to 27. They were clothed, given board and lodging, and brought up to go into service. Next door to the girls were the old men. Each had a room to himself and received clothes, shoes and linen plus a sum each week for food. The common room had a fire where they could do their own cooking, although this could be done for them. In 1836, there were 13 old men in the hospital. So Frome had the droll situation of having the boys and old women at the Blue House and the girls and old men at Keyford. Stevens' relations were much put out that Frome, as the recipient of such largesse, put up no monument to his memory, other than the inscription on the Hospital. They did so themselves in the Baptistry at St John's. On it is a good representation of Keyford Hospital. This distinctive building was pulled down in 1956, a decision much to be regretted. The road which ran beside it has now been called Stevens Lane in belated honour of a man whose generosity still helps to maintain the Blue House.

By 1810, the narrow lanes of Frome had caused the town to become a bottleneck for traffic as the roads which led to Frome had been widened and improved. The Market Place itself was almost cut in two by a house which sat in the middle, leaving a narrow aperture between it and the George. The road out was by Stony and Palmer Streets, to the entrance of St John's whence the traveller either went up Rook Lane (not the present one, but a lane which climbed the hill and came out in Behind Town at Rook Lane House), or Gentle Street, which was almost blocked by a building called The Folly (taken down in 1839), reducing the width to 10 ft. Either way was 'very narrow, steep, crooked and dangerous for travellers and carriages'. Some alighted and walked through Frome to avoid collision. Leading the campaign for improvement was Thomas Bunn, a solicitor who rarely practised, living at Monmouth House. He was born in 1767 and married one of the Kelson family, of Beckington. She died young and he devoted the rest of his life to making Frome a town of which he could be proud. This meant a classical town, for Bunn loved Greek and Roman art. His ideal was the Palladian stateliness of Bath although he wished Frome so far to surpass her mentor that people would speak of Bath, near Frome. Many tales are told of his generosity, such as the beggars who awaited him each morning and to whom he gave money, with his hand held behind him so that he could not see them. Bunn by no means achieved all his objectives and we must be glad that Frome has remained a genuine old cloth town, but his efforts did result in the cutting of Bath Street, a fine and fitting memorial. There was no trouble in raising the £10,000 required and the necessary enabling Act was passed in 1810. Bath Street, named after the Marquess of Bath, Lord Weymouth having been advanced to that dignity in 1789, was modelled on Union Street in Bath and in itself made a handsome carriage-way from the Market Place (which had been opened up by the destruction of the tenements in the middle) out of the town. It was also advantageous in that it resulted in the destruction of Anchor Barton, so-called from the Anchor Inn mentioned in the Church rates in 1677, an area above the Market Place with 'such an accumulation of dung-hills, slaughter-houses, and tallow-melting houses as to be indescribable'.

The new street was soon as 'civic' as Bunn could wish. By 1820 terraces of handsome houses descended to the Market Place. Bunn was instrumental in ornamenting some of them with pilasters, a classical motif, in setting up the arms of the Marquess of Bath, and in planting trees and shrubs including a surviving Cedar of Lebanon. In 1814, a new west front and screen were designed for St John's by Sir Jeffry Wyatville, later architect to George IV, but then working for the Marquess of Bath at Longleat. Rook Lane Chapel was refronted to give it a more imposing appearance, and in 1825, a National School was built to a Gothic revival design by Mr Finden, of Bath. This stood on the site of The Maltings and after being allowed to moulder for 30 years in the Frome fashion, was demolished in 1974. Bunn was also able to arrange improvements in other parts of the town. He persuaded Lord Cork to build an Assembly Room on the site of the George Inn stables, at the corner of Hill Lane, soon to be renamed Cork Street in honour of His Lordship. Underneath was another improvement, a covered market. Both are now occupied by the National Westminster Bank. Designed by Sir Jeffry Wyatville, in the style of the Greek revival, it is one of Frome's most notable buildings. The ornament is limited to Ionic columns and pilasters carrying a frieze and handsome cornice, sunken panels and window mouldings, capturing a 'Grecian' feeling of cool dignity and reserve. Bunn, given an inch, took a yard and showed Lord Cork an engraving of the Roman Forum 'as a good design for a modern market place'. Lord Cork 'thought of economy and said it would not pay'. The coronation of George IV was celebrated here in 1821 with a dinner 'of all the luxuries of the season'. The same year Frome Bridge was rebuilt, one side lined with two-storey houses, a rare, if not unique, feature. Bunn's most grandiose scheme for a Grecian crescent above Christchurch Street West never came to fruition. One of the four pillars which were to mark its entrance still stands in Wesley Slope and a second pillar has been erected next to Christ Church cemetery. It was to look down a vista through South to North Parade, an ideal that could only have been achieved by the destruction of much of the old town. Bunn lived until 1853, active and promoting improvement to the last. He is buried in Christchurch Cemetery, the grave being one he had thoughtfully provided for potential cholera victims, but when it was not required for this purpose, kept for himself. It has regularly been refurbished by the Frome Society for Local Study.

Despite this Augustan planning the Old Adam in Frome would out. There was another serious riot in 1813 during enrolment for the local militia. Those chosen for enlistment became disorderly and two were taken to the Guardhouse next to the Blue Boar. A mob came to the rescue and tried to take the roof off the Guardhouse. The Riot Act was read but the magistrates, including Lord Cork, received a severe buffeting before matters were brought under control. Lawlessness of this kind did not prevent another 'improvement': the abolition of the Pillory in 1814. The last to be punished in this was one Gideon Hill, who kept a house of ill-fame. He stood there from noon until four o'clock with his hands in clips, while the populace bombarded him with garbage. A more serious affair was the murder of Farmer William Webb, of Roddenbury Hill, in 1812. The culprits were two local men, George Ruddock and George Carpenter. Ruddock went to see Webb and was admitted by his servant, Mary Gibbons. 'Come in, George, and have some cider' invited the victim, to which Ruddock replied: 'No. I don't want cider. I want to go home and have some supper, as I am very *lier*' (to lie and wait) and instantly shot the farmer. The servant was hit on the head and thrown down a well. Both men were hanged at Warminster. Petty crime was dealt with by the Constable of Frome, and the diary of Isaac Gregory, who was Constable in 1817-18, survives and throws much light on the disorderly state of the town. Gregory, who was proud of his office, did his best to uphold its dignity and probity while exercising his authority with fairness, humanity and some humour. He was incensed when John Biggs, of Mells, in 'a dreadful passion at the Eagle' assaulted him—'a violent outrage on my person'—but withdrew the prosecution when, after taking Biggs to Orchardleigh, Justice Champneys told him to come back the next day. 'Extremely mortified,' wrote Gregory, 'at the *injustice* of a *justice*.' He was 'very much disgusted' when the Tithingman, who ought to have known better, 'was much overcome with liquor and was very insulting to a respectable man at the Blue Boar'. Champneys told Gregory 'to look sharp after a few of the most abandoned prostitutes... they are very numerous in the town... and begin with almost every man they meet'. He found some men at Mrs Morgan's who kept a house of ill-fame in Back (Eagle) Lane but she told him they were her cousins come to have a glass with her. He had more success with 'a bad creature called Bird' who had a relationship with John French, a clothier. Bird, a spirited lady 'gave him a deal of Tongue Pye' and was bold and undaunted before the magistrates. She was genteel and elegant and he and his deputy joked about his fine feathered bird, especially as the deputy had caught 'an fat old body'.

Gregory was constantly breaking up drunken fights. As there were 36 alehouses, which sold 6,700 hogsheads of strong beer each year, this is not surprising. The colliers, who brought coal by packhorse from Radstock, frequented the Packhorse Inn where they drank and quarrelled almost constantly, while 'lewd women' sang to them outside. A 'severe battle' in the lower Market Place started because one man struck another's cow on the horn. 'The farmers enjoyed it so much they would not send for the Constable.'

There was a Playhouse in Frome in 1817 at which Gregory had to sort out a 'terrible row', the actors fighting amongst themselves because the management had refused to let one of them have a good benefit. Thanks to the Constable, the play went on with the actors, alas, full of spleen towards each other. At the Frome Fair, Gregory had to deal with 'a great muster of pick-pockets from Bristol'. He disliked enforcing the Poor Rate 'when they themselves have had half bread to eat'. Stout boys at play on Sunday Gregory compelled to go to church, but when he caught a man drinking in the Griffin on the sabbath he put him in the stocks. Some arrested claimed they were 'much better fed in prison which made them much happier'. A boy stealing potatoes was sentenced to a month's hard labour; another was whipped through the town for robbing an orchard. One youth caught fighting was asked by the magistrate: 'What are you?' 'I do work in a well, Your Honour', came the reply. 'Well then' (magisterially) 'pray go in to the well and don't never appear above ground again'. Isaac Gregory, who served the office for his brother in return for a great coat, is a sympathetic figure who has left us a lively picture of Frome in his day.

The early 19th century was a time of poverty, distress, and discontent. Unemployment was blamed (with some reason) on the introduction of machinery. This meant the great clothiers needed fewer hands while many small clothiers (Thomas Bunn estimated the number at 50) went out of business. The banking crisis of 1825 also hit Frome, Willoughbys and Messiters being two of the firms that failed. William Cobbett, who visited Frome on his *Rural Rides* in 1826, blamed the inefficiency of the clothiers for the 'irretrievable decay of the place', claiming that the superfine black broadcloth offered to him at 30s a yard could be bought at home for 7s 6d. Local firms were not competing economically with the more completely mechanised northern factories. He thought Frome 'a little Manchester... it has all the *flash* of a Manchester, and the innkeepers.. .look and behave like Manchester fellows'. As he entered the town, he saw two or three hundred of the unemployed weavers cracking stones and moving earth to make a road, and in a fine piece of invective castigated the mill owners and rejoiced at their difficulties: 'Yes, these men have ground down into powder those who were earning them their fortunes; let the grinders themselves now be ground'. Increasing poverty led to acts of violence. One of Sheppard's stores in Pilly Vale was set on fire and a like fate overtook Humphries' factory in 1821 with the loss of steam engine, machinery and wool valued at £5,000. In 1792, £1,970 a year was spent on the poor, a figure which had risen to £11,723 by 1831. To many the workhouse with milk, onions, and broth for breakfast, and bread, cheese and beer for dinner (except Mondays and Thursdays when beef, veal, pork and vegetables were allowed) seemed like paradise. The high poor rates put a stop to building. One landlord in 1827 was glad to let a house for 10s a year, 400 in the town being empty. His agent wrote to him that there were 'seven shops vacant in Cheap Street, and God knows when they will be taken'. A charitable society of aristocratic ladies was set up, and cottage gardens provided, but these were only palliatives. A little money could be made by the poor through selling their urine to the clothiers, where it was used in the manufacture. It is a measure of how desperate matters were in Frome that 85 people were sent out to Canada in 1831 and 140 the following year, at the expense of the parish. The second wave was decimated by cholera at Quebec. The improvement of trade in the 1840s brought this grim period to a close.

Jeffries Mill, Spring Gardens.

ABOVE LEFT: Rawlings' cloth mill in Christchurch Street West, incorporating remains of the first factory in Frome, and BELOW: floods were a frequent occurence at Tuckers' mills at Wallbridge. ABOVE RIGHT: Keyford 'Home', completed in 1803, and BELOW: during demolition in 1957. BELOW: The school at Fromefield, built by the Sheppard family for their staff. (FM)

ABOVE: The most important improvement of the 19th century was Bath Street, cut in 1810, and CENTRE: The National School—part of the embellishment of Bath Street—built in 1825 and pulled down in 1974. LEFT: Pound note issued by the banking firm of N. Messiter & Co which failed in 1825.

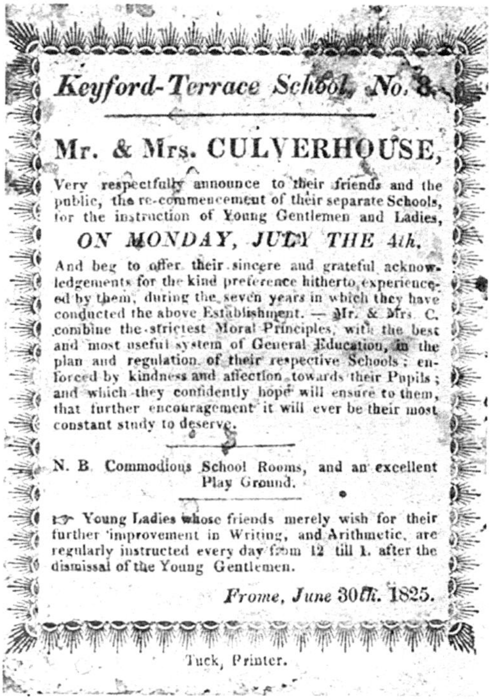

Keyford-Terrace School, No. 8.

Mr. & Mrs. CULVERHOUSE,

Very respectfully announce to their friends and the public, the re-commencement of their separate Schools, for the instruction of Young Gentlemen and Ladies,

ON MONDAY, JULY THE 4th.

And beg to offer their sincere and grateful acknowledgements for the kind preference hitherto experienced by them, during the seven years in which they have conducted the above Establishment. — Mr. & Mrs. C. combine the strictest Moral Principles, with the best and most useful system of General Education, in the plan and regulation of their respective Schools; enforced by kindness and affection towards their Pupils; and which they confidently hope will ensure to them, that further encouragement it will ever be their most constant study to deserve.

N. B. Commodious School Rooms, and an excellent Play Ground.

☞ Young Ladies whose friends merely wish for their further improvement in Writing, and Arithmetic, are regularly instructed every day from 12 till 1. after the dismissal of the Young Gentlemen.

Frome, June 30th. 1825.

Tuck, Printer.

ABOVE LEFT: Willoughby's grocers' shop as it was c1820; where Lloyd's Bank now stands. RIGHT: A Regency house: High Place, Keyford, another victim of road widening. CENTRE ABOVE: The Assembly Rooms, built in 1820 and used for public purposes until 1974, and BELOW: the Bridge, rebuilt in 1820, as drawn by David Grapes. (FM) BELOW LEFT: One pillar marks the intended entrance and a second has been erected at the other end next to Christ Church, to Thomas Bunn's crescent above Christchurch Street West, which was never completed . The Old Police Station was built in 1856 to a design by C.E. Davis, City Architect of Bath. RIGHT: Card advertising Mr & Mrs Culverhouse's private school in Keyford Terrace. (JWL)

ABOVE LEFT: The Market Place and Bath Street c1840, much as it was at the time of the Election Riot. (FM) RIGHT: Sir Henry Lopes, MP for Frome, from a 'Spy' cartoon. (BC) CENTRE LEFT: Lord Weymouth was acclaimed in Christchurch Street West after winning the Frome seat in the 1895 election. RIGHT: Christ Church c1900, (FM) and BELOW: East Woodlands School by Goodridge. (BC)

Progress and Reform

Frome may have been poor but she enjoyed a show and when William IV was proclaimed King on 8 July, 1830, there was a grand procession through the town 'not less than 17,000 persons assembled' according to W.P. Penny's diary—an impossibly high figure. The new reign ushered in an age of reform with a Whig ministry dedicated to the abolition of the 'rotten boroughs', those Parliamentary seats whose population had dwindled to next to nothing, and to enfranchising the larger centres of population. Under the Reform Act of 1832, Frome became a Parliamentary borough returning one member. The town with its puritan traditions was strongly in favour of reform but there was no serious trouble (as there was in Bristol) until the election itself. This took place on 10 December 1832, Thomas Sheppard standing for the Radicals while the Tories were represented by the popular but disreputable Sir Thomas Champneys, of Orchardleigh. The two men were personal enemies. When Champneys had been accused of sodomy in 1820, Sheppard had testified against him, which Champneys, in his lordly way, put down to 'recent opulence and modern pretension'. Voting was in public, with the hustings in Cork Street. The supporters of both sides were determined to assemble in force. Sir Thomas Champneys arrived with many hundreds of men and boys, some armed with bludgeons and cudgells loaded with lead, some on horseback, and immediately attacked Sheppard's supporters. Then Sheppard appeared, accompanied by 500 men, said to be unarmed. He ascended the hustings, but through the whole day was unable to make himself heard, his voice drowned by the clamour. He was also showered with sticks and stones and some of his friends had their coats ripped from their backs. Champneys made a long speech and was loudly cheered. Thomas Ford, one of Sheppard's supporters, was brutally beaten up and later died from his injuries.

So great was the violence that the magistrates decided to swear in special constables in an attempt to control the situation. This took place at the George Inn, which was promptly attacked by the mob. They were driven out after fierce fighting in which several people were seriously injured and the bar destroyed. The mob besieged the inn and smashed the windows. Sheppard prudently withdrew to Fromefield House which was guarded by 300 men, and a troop of Dragoons was summoned from Trowbridge to Beckington, to be on call if required. Polling began amid scenes of continued violence and destruction. Early on the second day, Sheppard had gained 163, more than one half of those entitled to vote. This infuriated the supporters of Sir Thomas who, crying 'Champneys for ever', attacked the Crown Inn, through which they hoped to get into the George and so at Sheppard's supporters. After fierce fighting they were driven back, and a space cleared before the two inns, the special constables being showered with missiles and bleeding profusely. The Riot Act was read and those constables who possessed carbines were ordered to fire. Two of the leading rioters were wounded. About three o'clock, the Dragoons entered Frome and put a stop to the battle. Champneys' vigorous attempt to intimidate the electors had failed. He retired to Orchardleigh and sent in his resignation. The final result was Sheppard, 163; Champneys, 100. There had been much damage to life and limb as well as to property. Luke Perman, a draper, claimed compensation from the Hundred of Frome for the total destruction of his house in the Market Place. Thomas Sheppard won three subsequent elections in less dramatic circumstances and remained MP for Frome until 1847. Sir Thomas Champneys, the last of his line, died in 1839, a talking point to the end, his ornate coffin displayed in Frome to the wonder of the inhabitants. Frome retained its own MP until 1885, when the seat was merged with the division. The town usually returned a Liberal. These included members of the Boyle family of Marston, Thomas Hughes, author of *Tom Brown's School Days*, and Sir Henry Lopes.

Two great personages visited Frome at this period. One was Nicholas I, Tsar and Autocrat of All the Russias, who returning from Longleat to London via Bath, the nearest railway station, in 1844 came through the town. It was a Sunday and crowds hurried from church and chapel as the carriage containing the Russian monarch came down Bath Street and stopped outside the George. The visit must have been unexpected for it was some time before the innkeeper, the 'manly and dignified' Edward Brunsdon, who had himself been in service at Longleat, appeared and handed His Imperial and Royal Majesty, whom Queen Victoria found 'a very striking man; still very handsome,' a glass of sherry. The cavalcade then drove off, leaving the by-standers with the impression that they had seen the finest man in Europe. The second visitor was the Prince of Wales, the future Edward VII, who as a boy of 12 stayed at the Crown, which was considered quieter than the George. The prince's tutor was given a napkin, but the waiter did not think it worthwhile to waste one on the little boy. The pair were travelling incognito on one of the prince's country tours.

The early 19th century was by no means stagnant in Frome. If the bodies of the poor were neglected, much thought was given to their souls. Christ Church was built in 1818 on land given by Sir Thomas Champneys. The original church was designed by G.A. Underwood 'celebrated for nothing, but having made some improvements in Shepton Mallet gaol', according to Thomas Bunn (actually he was County Surveyor and designed Frome Bridge). Little remains of his church but the tower, for it was successfully enlarged in a more correct Perpendicular style by Manners & Gill, of Bath, in 1849-51. Belatedly, the large working population of St Katherine's Manor was also given a church, which gave a new name to the area, Holy Trinity. This was paid for by public subscription, designed by H.E. Goodridge, of Bath, and built in 1837-38. The building was functional, not particularly mediaeval, and had the altar at the West End, a combination which would have been unthinkable a few years later. Bunn says that Goodridge never saw the site and was merely told to design a front which would look well from the street, and in this he succeeded. At the opening ceremony, Sir Thomas Champneys appeared in a long robe and staff, officiating in person as hereditary Sexton of Frome. Two ghastly (in the true sense of the word, deathlike) paintings of *The Entombment* and *The Crucifixion* were given to the new Church by Henry Thomas Ryall (1811-1867), the son of a Frome grocer and a talented artist and draughtsman, who became 'Portrait and Historical Engraver to Her Majesty', Queen Victoria. Later Holy Trinity acquired a whole set of Morris glass from designs by Sir Edward Burne-Jones. In 1844, the chancel and St Andrew's chapel at St John's were restored as a memorial to Bishop Ken. The Primitive Methodists erected their chapel in Sun Street in 1834 and the Irvingites established themelves in the Old Presbytery which was taken over by the Roman Catholics as St Catharine's Church in 1853.

Education was not neglected. Church schools were built at East Woodlands (designed by Goodridge), Christ Church (said to be by George Gilbert Scott, but if so, uninspired) and Holy Trinity, while there were four schools attached to St John's. Milk Street School was founded on the site of a chapel in 1843 and by 1855 had 116 boys and 99 girls. Bunn noted of Holy Trinity School in 1840 that: 'Revd. Alfred Daniel is about to build a school; but seems to have as little knowledge of the affair he undertakes as his predecessor (Revd. J.B.B. Clarke) who built the Church At Holy Trinity Parsonage. The Daniel Press was founded by the children of the curate, destined to acquire a reputation as 'a private press of considerable note' with 'a distinctive and honourable place among its compeers'. C.H.O. Daniel, who later entered the church and became Provost of Worcester College, Oxford, started the press with his brothers for personal pleasure. He continued, so as to be able to print special literature and to please literary friends. He also aimed to improve printing and book production and in this respect his press was a forerunner of the more famous Kelmscott Press. Printings from the Frome period, 1845 to 1863 with occasional productions up to 1870, are collectors' items. They consist mostly of minor pieces, tickets, letters, texts of sermons, and prayers interesting for their local associations and for the artistry of their typography and ornamental devices. The mark of the press was Daniel in the lions' den, from a woodcut by Alfred Parsons, the Beckington-born artist, and a relation.

The Daniel Press flourished side by side with two rather larger, commercial printers. Crockers, who had done most of Frome's printing for the previous 30 years, sold their business to W.P. Penny for £500 in 1832. Penny had come from Exeter to Frome in 1820 and married Martha Carpenter, of Pear Tree Cottage, Rodden. Here they had as their lodger the curate (later of Buckland Dinham and Frome also) Rev E.B. Ramsay, afterwards the famous Dean of Edinburgh, who was to look back on his years of 'useful, cheerful, happy employment at Frome' as among the happiest of his life. The Pennys later lived in the Old Church House whence they could step across the garden into their printing and bookselling business at 8, Bath Street. Penny's son, William Carpenter Penny, (1822-1887), was a prominent Frome townsman and founded the short-lived Conservative newspaper, *The Frome Times* as well as printing Vicar Bennett's *History of the Old Church of St John of Froome*. Penny was a microscopical expert, while his collection of mediaeval locks and keys was said to be the finest in England. The business continued under the direction of his family until after 1900. As printers Pennys were overshadowed by the new firm of Butler and Tanner. This famous firm owes its origin to William Langford, a Berkshire man who had been apprenticed to a chemist but had a keen interest in printing and publishing. He came to Frome in 1840 and rented a chemist's shop at 20 Bath Street (it had been started in 1820 and remained a chemist's until 1975) where his patent medicines became well-known. Langford also started a printing works, but found it impossible to cope with the two businesses, and summoned W.T. Butler, once a fellow apprentice in his uncle's pharmacy in High Wycombe, to his aid. Butler handled the printing side of the business which began humbly enough in the adjoining yard of the Wheatsheaves Inn.

At the end of 1846, Langford and Butler published *The Frome Almanac*, which survived until 1947 and forms an invaluable record of the town, its people and its trade through a hundred changing years. In 1854, they printed and published *The Frome Sentinel*, which the following year was incorporated in *The Somerset and Wilts Journal*, an excellent local paper in the Liberal interest, which survived until after the First World War and is now incorporated in *The Somerset Standard.* Having laid the foundations of a printing empire of whose ultimate size he could hardly have dreamed, Langford retired to West-End where he lived another 50 years. The chemist's shop at 20 Bath Street was taken over by William Brett Harvey, a dedicated nonconformist and teetotaller who played an influential role in the life of the town. Harvey continued to publish the *Journal,* but it was printed by Butler and his new partner, Joseph Tanner. They had now outgrown the old premises behind the Wheatsheaves and moved to a shed in the garden of Castle House, Butler's home in Castle Street. By 1866, Butler and Tanner claimed to be the largest printing works in the West of England, and began to build the Selwood Printing Works to a neo-Byzantine design, much favoured for industrial structures, by Joseph Chapman jr, the Frome architect and sculptor whose father had built the screen across St John's forecourt. The printing works were completed in three stages in 1866, 1870, and 1876.

A new workhouse, now the Selwood Hospital, had been erected after the passing of the Poor Law Amendment Act in 1834. This had grouped Frome and the surrounding parishes into a Union run by a Board of Guardians. There had been a workhouse in Frome at least since 1733, when a child from it, 'name not known', had been baptised. In 1750, the Vestry had leased for 21 years a property of Lord Cork at Welshmill called Brocas' Barton. They then bought in 1779 a dyehouse (where Clumber House now stands) which had belonged to Thomas Jesser, and this, with six attached cottages, remained the workhouse until 1838, when it was sold to a maltster called Joseph Oxley. The new building was crowded and ill-ventilated, nearly all the beds touching each other. Sometimes 350 people were resident and in the early days when there was an epidemic, the sick could not be separated from the healthy, and many died.

'The trade of Frome has been declining for some years' declared the Imperial Gazetteer in 1843. New industries, however, reduced its dependence on wool. Gas lighting was introduced in 1831, Mr Penny lighting his shop in Bath Street with it for the first time on 10 November that year. This 'made' the firm of Edward Cockey and Sons Ltd, whose main manufactures were now to be gas holders and standards, although they also made steam engines, boilers, pillars, and iron roofs. They made the iron pillars and railings on Coalash Walk to protect the public, when the Prince and Princess of Wales visited Longleat in 1881 and left from Frome Station. A more famous firm, which still flourishes in Frome, although now making hot pressings and castings for the engineering industry, is J.W. Singer. John Webb Singer, the founder of the firm about 1848, was originally a watchmaker in Bath Street. He took up hot metal work more or less as a hobby, being interested in antique metal work and jewellery. By 1866, he was making 'mediaeval' furnishings, mostly for ecclesiastical purposes in silver, brass and iron, employing 15 to 20 hands. He supplied more than 100 churches and made hundreds of candlesticks, many for Oxford colleges, and experimented with enamelled mediaeval jewellery. From altar rails, standards, screens, gates and brackets, Singer evolved to such famous national monuments as the Boadicea group on the Embankment (one of whose horses was hoisted on a cart and drawn by five horses up Bath Street in the Diamond Jubilee procession of Queen Victoria). After J.W. Singer's death in 1904, Singers cast Edward VII, in Waterloo Place, London; Captain Scott, and the panels of the Scottish National War Memorial in Edinburgh Castle. The statuary foundry was sold off in 1926. Towards the end of his life, Singer, who found the 17th century houses of Gentle Street inconvenient, bought the 'spacious Knoll House, which had been built in 1839 with an eye to modern comfort by Dr Bush for his son. Singer's son, Edgar, left it to the Royal British Legion in 1947. It has now been converted to housing.

Among the textile firms, two stand out. Thompson's silk works was in Merchant's Barton. Thompson, a Londoner and a Baptist, came to Frome from Shacklewell in 1845 and by 1851 employed 348 women and children, running an 'extensive silk trade with skill, success, and liberality' in Thomas Bunn's opinion. Before he died in 1873, Thompson took into partnership Philip le Gros, who went to live at North Hill House where his daughter continued to reside until 1955, when she sold it to Frome Urban District Council. Philip le Gros married Elizabeth, the daughter of John Sinkins and so became connected with one of Frome's great characters, whom le Gros consistently annoyed by always insisting on being referred to formally as Mr le Gros. John Sinkins (1805-1869) was a kindly, friendly, and generous man, very much hail-fellow-well-met, a John Bull type both mentally and physically. His mother ran a drapers' shop in the Market Place which her only son cordially detested. However, luck was with him. He married Eliza Stancomb, the wealthy daughter of a Trowbridge clothier, while his sister married Thomas Green, son of a Nottingham lace manufacturer and an astute businessman. Sinkins thus acquired money and sound advice at a stroke. He and Green became fast friends as well as business colleagues and were ultimately buried in the same grave in Vallis Way Cemetery.

On Green's advice, Sinkins went into partnership with Levi Wood, taking over the Hapsford Mill, which had been run with outstanding success by George George ('the handsomest and healthiest of all our 12,000 inhabitants' according to Bunn) who had made a fortune of £70,000 there. In 1859, they moved to Staplemead Mill. Sinkins and Wood made cloth for livery coats for the servants of the aristocracy and for the linings of carriages, being careful to preserve 'the old tints of colour which have become the hereditary pride of many noble families'. Sinkins made a fortune and knew how to spend it. His bluff humour was legendary, and it is said that when a new curate, Mr Dove Dove, arrived wearing a long black gown with a band round the waist, Sinkins went up to him and asked: 'Excuse me, my friend, but are you a man or a woman?' He was much involved in bringing the railway to Frome and made a profit on this too, selling to the GWR the land on which Frome Station was built, for £1,800, when he had bought it for only a few hundreds. The Station was opened on 7 October 1850, amid a singular lack of enthusiasm. An excursion to Oxford cost 3s 6d and the trip to Paddington took 41/2 hours. The station was designed in the office of I.K. Brunel and is a largely unaltered example of a small station of the period. The train shed, covering both tracks, is probably the last survivor in use in the West of England and the earliest remaining in Britain. It was well restored by British Rail in 1982. Sinkins, who lived in some style at Wallbridge House, became chairman of Frome magistrates.

Sinkins will be remembered for his gift to the town of the Literary and Scientific Institution. This remarkable building in the round-windowed Venetian style, cleverly fitted into a wedge-shaped site from which it seems to sail boldly towards the town, was designed by J. Hine, a relative of Sinkins, in 1868. It cost £3,000, more than £80,000 in today's money, all of which Sinkins paid.. The Lit., as it came to be known, has recently been cleaned, an exercise which has brought out the intrinsic merit of the building. It housed a literary and scientific society founded in 1844, apparently after 30 years of debate. Bunn says it was the most popular society in the town and it received presents of books, stuffed birds, fossils, and many items of local interest. Unfortunately, in a later period of neglect, many important relics were lost or destroyed; it now houses Frome Museum.

A report on the sanitary condition of Frome by Sir Henry de la Beche before 1845 found the houses of the poor substantial and generally occupied by only one family, although lodgers were often taken in. The people were 'under-fed and averse to ventilation'. There were no back-to-back houses. There were no baths and the river was unfit for bathing because the water was filthy, the flow obstructed by the weirs and dams of the clothiers. Flooding was a constant hazard. Neither street cleansing nor a sewage system existed. There was no public water supply (until 1880), people using springs and wells. The death rate each year was above the national average, tradesmen having the least life expectancy.

The age of Victorian improvement had now set in. Improvement, not only of streets and buildings, but also of minds and stock, was the order of the day. An Agricultural Society was in existence by 1835 and in 1859 was holding a show each year about a fortnight before Christmas. In 1871,under the influence of Robert Porteous, the steward of the Earl of Cork and Orrery, it was decided to hold 'an Annual Cheese Show and Fair on an extended scale', the model being the Kilmarnock Show in Porteous' native Scotland. So the Frome Cheese Fair was born, still one of the highlights of the year. In 1978, in a pleasant Frome way, it celebrated its centenary, although it was neither the 100th show nor the 100th anniversary of the Society.

The Mechanics Institute was founded in 1858 on the corner of Eagle Lane with a library of 1400 volumes, lectures and meetings. John Webb Singer with the support of the artistic Mrs E.V. Boyle, wife of the Rector of Marston Bigot, founded the School of Art, 'in connection with the Science and Art Department, South Kensington', originally situated in North Parade, but later moving to Park Road. The new confidence found expression in the Art and Industrial Exhibition, organised by Singer and Penny in 1866. The exhibits included a loom and steam machinery, a printing press, glass, pictures, Frome marbles, cups, vases, silver, Sir Walter Raleigh's watch, and a glass hive, being generally held to be most amusing. In 1871, on leaving Marston, Mr and Mrs Boyle gave the cross and fountain which still stand in the Market Place, as a token of affection. When Thomas Bunn had attempted this, the heavy vase he had erected for the fountain was taken away in the night, thrown into the river and smashed. Today, the Boyle fountain is a flower bed, having been used on market days to wash fish. Frome Market Place does not seem destined to enjoy water in any ornamental form.

None of these improvements caused such remark as the restoration of St John's Church by Rev W.J.E. Bennett in 1860-66. Bennett, a High Churchman and follower of the Anglo-Catholic Oxford movement, a devotee of ritual and ceremony, had been driven out of his London church, St Paul's, Knightsbridge, by the storm which followed the restoration of the Roman Catholic hierarchy in England in 1850, an action much resented by protestant opinion, for which it was thought the ritualistic practices of Bennett and his friends had paved the way. The Marchioness of Bath, who sympathised with his views, offered him the Vicarage of Frome in 1852. He gratefully accepted and devoted himself to the problems of a crumbling church which he eventually rebuilt, practically stone by stone, at a cost of £40,000, little short of a million pounds today. The architect was C.E. Giles, of London, and the builders the local firm of Frederick and George Brown. Bennett himself wrote the story of the restoration and its symbolism in *The Old Church of St. John of Froome* and the present writer has described it in some detail in *Light in Selwood*. In its day, St John's was 'famous for the beauty, richness and completeness of its fittings and furniture' and one of the 'sights' for distinguished visitors such as Benjamin Disraeli who found it 'marvellous; exquisitely beautiful and...in admirable taste'. The ornamental work and carving by J. Forsyth is remarkable, particularly the *Via Crucis*, six episodes on the road to Calvary over the north porch, an astonishing feature in an English parish church. With the increasing interest in, and appreciation of Victorian architecture, St John's Church is greatly admired as an outstanding example of its *genre*. Bennett himself outlived his early unpopularity and died, greatly honoured and respected, in 1886.

Hansom cabs awaiting the arrival of a train at Frome Station in 1900. (FSLS)

126

ABOVE LEFT: An artist's impression of Holy Trinity as originally designed by Goodridge. RIGHT: Primitive Methodist Sunday School in Whittox Lane. (GHH) CENTRE: Milk Street School in 1897. (BC) BELOW LEFT: Bookplate of J.W. Singer showing Knoll House where he lived during the last years of his life. RIGHT: Butler and Tanner's printing works, c1860. (FM)

ABOVE LEFT: Thomas Green as a young man. (FSLS) CENTRE: J.W. Singer's shop in the Market Place c1870. RIGHT: Rev E.B. Ramsey, Curate of Frome and later Dean of Edinburgh. (BC) CENTRE LEFT: John Sinkins in 1867—John Bull style. RIGHT: Fashionable writing paper of 1870 was headed with this sketch of St John's, (FM) and BELOW: the restoration of St John's was in progress in the early 1860s. (FM)

ABOVE: Singer's bronze foundry before 1900. (FM) BELOW: The Public Offices were built for the Board of Guardians in 1891.

ABOVE LEFT: The Literary and Scientific Institution was built in the Venetian style in 1868. (FM) RIGHT: A Victorian beauty: Mrs Richard Boyle, from a painting by Sir William Boxall. (GHB) BELOW LEFT: The Mechanics Institute at the corner of Church Slope and Eagle Lane when newly built in 1858. It is now demolished. CENTRE: One of the many sculptures by James Forsyth in St John's. (JWL) RIGHT: A glimpse of the Art and Industrial Exhibition held in Frome in 1866. (GHB)

Frome at War

In 1878 one of Frome's strongest links with the past was broken when Sheppards' great complex of factories closed. The buildings soon fell into ruin and were used as a quarry to build cottages. The Sheppards do not appear to have adapted quickly enough to changing fashion. The shiny black broadcloth which never wore out sounds a dreary material, and even the farmers ceased to buy their market suits of Sheppard's plaid, a bale of which, untouched for many years, was seen by a Frome man at a country drapers' in 1900. As late as 1866, Sheppards had been producing 5,000 yards of cloth a week. Now the business went north. Sheppards dropped behind and never recovered. By 1900 even the family had disappeared from Frome. A smaller Firm, Magill & Stephens, woollen manufacturers, who had taken over the Wallbridge Mills, failed in 1868, but was bought by a Trowbridge cloth dealer, W.H. Tucker. His son Alfred, who lived at Keyford House, ran a successful and expanding business and the buildings were greatly enlarged. Wallbridge Mills operated until 1965, their closure bringing the long story of the wool industry in Frome to an end and the site has been used for industrial units and housing.

The old partnership of Manor Court and Vestry which had governed Frome for so long was now giving way to newer authorities. The Board of Guardians had been functioning since 1834 and in 1891 built the Public Offices in 'Renaissance' style to house their administration. They were joined in 1865 by a Local Board, whose leading member was Alderman Flatman, a Suffolk man who ran a college in Keyford, one of the private schools with which Frome abounded in the late 19th century. Flatman, whose name is constantly recalled to Frome people by the clock on the Public Offices, lately restored to use, was Chairman of the Local Board for ten years and a leading influence in establishing the waterworks, a sewage scheme, a Cottage Hospital (in Castle House), and a recreation ground. When Flatman died in 1894 *The Somerset and Wilts Journal* declared that he was one of Frome's few public men 'who have left their mark upon its history and bequeathed to posterity a record of noble deeds nobly done'. Flatman's achievements were not exactly exciting, but did much to improve living conditions.

The Lord of the Manor, the ninth Earl of Cork and Orrery from 1856 until 1904, was an influential figure. He was also Lord Lieutenant of Somerset and lived at Marston House in some style. The Countess of Cork never ventured into Frome except in a carriage drawn by four horses ridden by postillions. There is a record of the Manor Court meeting at the George in 1839, and seven years earlier, James Vaters had possessed the resounding title of High Constable of the Hundred of Frome. There was still a Bailiff of the Hundred in 1875 but none is recorded after this date. The reason is to be found in an Act of 1867, which deprived the Hundred Court of all real power, while an Act of 1886 removed the liability of the Hundred to be responsible for damage caused by riot, a liability of which the Hundred of Frome had been made painfully aware after the Election Riot of 1832. The Sheriff's tourn was abolished in 1887. The Market rights, which had been jealously guarded by the Lords of the Manor for so long, were sold by Lord Cork to the Frome Market Company in 1875. The manorial system was to all intents and purposes dead when, in 1905, the 10th Earl of Cork sold his property in Frome in lots, so giving it the coup de grace.

A hundred years ago Frome was still close to its mediaeval past. The town had not yet burst out of its ancient bounds. Nunney and Weymouth Roads were still country lanes, there was little building on Lock's Hill and behind Wallbridge House lay fields and gardens. The fine old building firm of Sewards had not yet developed the Butts, nor Hodders built Badcox Parade. Somerset and Oakfield Roads were also developed by Sewards, but not until after the Park was opened in 1887. Neither Alexandra and Woodland Roads nor Summer Hill existed. The fair had not yet been brought under control or regulation. It sprawled all over the town, down Cork Street and up Cheap Street. Cheese was pitched on straw outside the churchyard gates, and cattle tied to any convenient railing or pillar in the streets. Sheep were penned near the Bridge and horses showed off their paces in the roads. There was a raised area of cobble stones where the Boyle Cross now stands. Here there were shooting galleries, stalls for toys and gingerbread, butter and eggs.

What is perhaps hardest to recapture is the smell of old Frome. It reeked of horses which were stabled 'anywhere and everywhere', leading to plagues of flies which congregated round the butchers and fishmongers, who employed boys with birch whisks to keep them off. Every street had its own smell, such as Lower Keyford, the seat of a tannery since the 17th century, the approach of whose workers 'could be scented afar off'. The clothworkers also had a strong aroma and this mixed with that of tallow chandlers and earth closets. Roads were ankle-deep in mud in winter or wet weather, and carpeted with dust in the summer. Shops were modest in size with small-paned windows. There were no motor cars of course, although one or two horse 'buses existed, and two-wheeled hansom cabs plied between the Station and the George and Bull's Hotel (the present Post Office) in the Market Place. The first garage in Frome was opened by Mr. Hobbs next to the Victoria Inn, Christchurch Street East, in 1907. Old recreations were still enjoyed: a performing bear, or a wild man in an iron cage fed on live rats (feeding time cost 6d extra). The River Frome flooded often and seriously, causing widespread damage. In the great flood of 1882 the waters reached as far as the Angel and Crown Inns, was 7 ft deep at Tucker's Mill and reached to the gates of Styles Hill House, the old home of the Sheppards and Edgells. This hazard by water continued until the river bed was deepened, realigned and embanked in 1969.

Under the Local Government Act of 1894, a sober Urban District Council was imposed on this earthy scene. *The Somerset Standard*, which had been founded in the Conservative interest in 1886, declared that it would 'rise Phoenix-like out of the ashes of the present Local Board'. The surrounding parishes were grouped in a Rural District Council which included Selwood, and so a large part of the old parish of Frome. Those two authorities, created when society was still dependent on the horse for local transport, endured through all the changes of the next 80 years, a fine example of English conservatism. The first Urban District Council consisted of 15 members and included Charles Baily, a wine merchant, J.W. Singer, Joseph Tanner, the printer, E.G. Ames, a solicitor, who became the first chairman, Henry and Samuel Rawlings, manufacturers, John Hodder, a builder, and Joseph Chapman, who described himself modestly as a marble worker. In 1901, there was another riot arising out of a strike at Butler and Tanners. Recorded a liberal minded magistrate, Rev W.A. Duckworth, of Orchardleigh, '8 young men....were found guilty of disturbance of the peace - much to their surprise'. They were sentenced to spells of six to eight weeks in prison with hard labour. 'Severe but necessary', commented Duckworth, 'they were free to strike and leave the factory, but not to interfere with fresh hands from a distance brought in by Mr Tanner to fill their places.' A happier occasion was the relief of Mafeking during the Boer War in May, 1900, which 'produced an outburst of patriotism as spontaneous as it was sincere'. The news, brought by the railway workers, led to a grand demonstration: bands played, bells rang, hooters were blown and a cheering procession of 3,000 people invaded the streets. In the evening 5,000 people assembled in the Market Place and sang patriotic songs to the accompaniment of a string band on the George balcony. The Vicar, the rather grand Rev W.F.H. Randolph, addressed the crowd: 'just as in a sense we are of one family in Frome so English people are united by the strongest possible tie, and though world wide it is pleasant to feel that we have a great Imperial destiny to fulfill' (cheers).

The mammoth reign of Queen Victoria was thought worthy of public commemoration; Frome benefited by two splendid amenities, the Victoria Baths and the Victoria Hospital. The building of the Leisure Centre in 1974 led to the closure of the old baths the following year to the regret of many who regarded them with affection. Provided under pressure from 'the working classes', the baths cost £1500; the pool was 75 by 30 feet. When opened by the Hon. Mrs. Duckworth (who thought them beautiful) the baths were regarded as amongst the finest in England.

The Duckworths of Orchardleigh were also deeply involved in the provision of the new hospital which opened in 1901 at a cost of £5000. The Revd. W.A. Duckworth provided £1000 as well as the architect, B. Vaughan Johnson, a relative, whose fees he paid. Mrs. Duckworth opened the Hospital's door with a golden key 'a token that at all times hereafter by day or by night it should be open for the relief of suffering and sickness'.

With these and other assets, Frome faced the new century in modest affluence and good order after 13 years of constant improvement. The town was largely self sufficient. The population was rising again. Taking Selwood into account, a parish created in 1894 out of the rural area of Frome, the population was 12027, a rise of 563 since 1891 and 847 since 1881.

Trade was satisfactory, businessmen enterprising, and public life vigorous with flourishing Conservative and Liberal Associations. Frome had its poor district in the Trinity area, nicknamed Chinatown, but there was much new housing going up in its 'salubrious suburbs' around Somerset Road and the Butts. The Urban and Rural District Councils met at leisure once a month in the Public Offices. The U.D.C. had five committees but the R.D.C. seems to have been able to do without any.

There were five Anglican churches. St. John's was headed by Prebendary Randolph to whom boys doffed their caps and girls curtsied. He was vicar from 1899 to 1938. A great churchman, he had some quirky ideas nevertheless. Living in the middle of Frome, he believed his nearest neighbours were the Duckworths at Orchardleigh. He forbade smoking in the churchyard as it was consecrated ground. Holy Trinity had its own cricket club. The nine nonconformist chapels were well supported; several had young peoples' groups and Badcox Lane its own football team. There was a Roman Catholic Church and a Salvation Army Citadel which was visited by General Booth in 1906, the great man staying at 'Belmont' in Weymouth Road.

Local children had a choice of eight council and church schools. There were also good private schools such as Selwood at Wine Street House, run by the Coombes family, and Keyford College, said to have been founded in 1803. Edwin Mann, the headmaster, entertained his pupils with stories of past wars in a cap and gown green with age, a benign figure compared to his wife whom they found terrifying. Higher education was dealt with at the School of Art and Science, founded in 1902. Here afternoon and evening classes were held. There was also the Mechanic's Institute on Church Slope and the Scientific and Literary Institution with a museum in North Parade.

A huge maltings built by the Baily family at the station in 1896 serviced the busy breweries which in turn served 56 public houses. There were six public halls and three masonic lodges. The Dramatic and Operatic Society was founded in 1904. Sport was well catered for with rugby, football, golf, hockey, swimming, quoits, and coursing clubs. Then as now the highlight of the year was the cheese show and carnival. The show was then held in the market yard and across the river in Singer's field. The 1906 show had 829 entries, considered a record.

The Whitsun processions with the distribution of buns was also an event much looked forward to. A new entertainment was the silent film. These were shown at the Auction Mart (Dore's) and later at the renowned Palace Cinema at the bottom of Church Steps. Local life was enlivened by a strong military presence, detachments of the Somerset Imperial Yeomanry, the Somerset Light Infantry, and the Cornwall & Somerset Royal Army Medical Corps being stationed in or near the town.

The military gave dignity to processions and funerals which often took place in Christchurch Street West, Frome's civic thoroughfare. The Volunteer Fire Brigade also took part in these events. The brigade had been founded as early as 1828 and was admired for its efficiency and handsome helmets.

At this time the motor car began to make its appearance on the Frome scene, although the roads were still primitive and untreated, dusty in Summer and muddy in winter. Dr. Wood, of Bridge House, seems to have possessed the first car, an Oldsmobile, in 1903. Other notables followed his example including Captain Phayre Ryall, of Critchill House, known as a Jehu. By 1908, Butler & Tanner had a Daimler lorry. Hobbs & Co opened Frome's first garage in 1907.

Two firms in Frome claimed to be motor manufacturers. The first was Eastmead & Biggs in Christchurch Street East. Then, from 1903 to 1909, the Frome Selwood Motor Works at Butts Hill produced the eight horse power 'Achilles', one of which still exists in good order. It was noted for its hill climbing capabilities. In fact, the components of these cars were brought in and they were merely put together in Frome. Despite this, the horse was still king. Every shopkeeper kept a horse and gig and the farmers came into market in horse drawn traps. Boys could earn a penny by holding the horses.

The Post Office was in No 6 Bath Street, where it had moved from Vicarage Street. The Postmen are to be seen in old photographs taking part in processions as a group. They dealt with nine dispatches of mail in a day and made four deliveries. It was not until 1915 that the Post Office moved down to the Market Place in what had been the Bull Hotel.

A new means of communication was becoming increasingly common: the telephone. It crept in, not at first in private houses but in the offices of doctors, industrialists and businessmen. Gas lighting, which had been present in Frome since 1831, disappeared in 1904 to be replaced by electricity. The impression of bustle and progress is underlined by the 1907 'Little Guide' to Somerset which describes Frome as a thriving town which did a brisk trade in woollen cloth, beer, printing and art metal products.

The 'art metal products' were a modest description of the fine statues produced by John Webb Singer, who died in 1904, at his foundry in Cork Street. These included the famous group of Boadicea in her chariot on the Thames Embankment, the dragon on Cardiff City Hall, the gates of Cliveden, Edward VII, the Captain Scott as well as many others.

The century opened with Britain in the midst of the Boer war. The relief of Mafeking in May, 1900, was greeted with incredible enthusiasm. A procession of 3000 people took to the streets, cheering and singing. Bells, hooters and bands added to the noise. In the evening, 5000 people gathered to sing patriotic songs in the Market Place. To cheers the vicar referred to 'our great Imperial destiny'. At Badcox, Mafeking Terrace still recalls that happy day.

The death of Queen Victoria in January, 1901 was commemorated with solemnity in Frome. It created a break with the past obvious to all. Nevertheless, a greater impact was made by the sudden death, in June, 1904, of the ninth Earl of Cork and Orrery, of Marston House. Popular and respected, a noted huntsman who once brought the Royal Buckhounds to Marston, he had been a good friend to Frome for more than 50 years.

Cork's son, the 10th Earl, disliked Marston and did not care for the country, preferring London life. The Marston estate was also mortgaged. He decided to sell everything in 1905, including the George Hotel and all the house property and building plots in Frome. The Marquess of Bath was also gradually parting with his town property in Frome so the economic links between the town and two great estates were largely severed. Today, only the cross given to the town in 1871 by the Hon. and Revd. Richard Boyle, and the name Cork Street remind us of our link with this famous family.

The even tenor of events was punctuated by more memorable happenings. The General Election of 1906 was well fought in Frome with the sitting Liberal M.P., Sir John Barlow, having a majority of 1745 over the Conservative, Charles Foxcroft. The next year the first carnival procession was staged. In 1909, the Prince and Princess of Wales came to Frome on their way back to London from Longleat. They caught a train at Frome Station but people were disappointed that they drove through in closed cars (despite the hot weather) and did not stop.

Perhaps the most unusual visitor was the Hon. J.S.T. McGowen, Prime Minister of New South Wales. He came in July, 1911, to plant one of two coronation oaks in Victoria Park. Lord Bath planted the other. George V and Queen Mary had just been crowned. The Premier's visit was also in honour of James Mario Matra. Matra was regarded by some as the founder of Australia. He was the first to suggest that a colony should be established there, although he did not envisage it as a convict settlement. The town of Matraville in New South Wales is named after him. Frome and Matraville exchanged flags. Some 5000 people visited Victoria Park to see the trees.

It was and is believed in Australia that Matra was a Frome man and a modern plaque recalls this. The origin of this curious myth may be the fact that Matra stayed with Lord Cork at Marston House in 1784. This appears to be his sole connection with Frome; he was born in New York. The outbreak of the First World War on 4th August 1914, took Frome by surprise; there was more interest in the suicide of a woman at Frome Station by throwing herself under the Weymouth train. But the town rallied and put itself on a war footing. Horses were commandeered for the army and a Territorial Company formed as well as emergency corps known as Tanner's Own from its commander, R.R. Tanner.

A recruiting meeting added 38 soldiers to the army. Billeted in the town were 1400 troops. Recreation rooms were opened for them in public buildings and the Keyford Asylum turned into a military hospital. Church parades accompanied by the Town Band enlivened the town as did recruitment meetings such as that held by Oliver Brooks from Midsomer Norton who had won a V.C. in France. This attracted a large crowd. A meeting to consider employing women in agriculture, however, met with 'an apathetic reception'.

Refugees from Belgium were welcomed with open arms, offers of hospitality and entertainment being general. Singers went over to making munitions, taking over the Market Hall and turning 23,000 tons of metal into shell cases. There was a scare about spies poisoning the water supply on orders from the Kaiser. Special guards watched the springs. Australian troops were quartered in Seward's yard. There was a blackout for fear of raids by Zeppelins.

Despite the carnage in France and such events as the sinking of the 'Lusitania' which caused 'considerable excitement' in Frome, local life continued, societies met, the Post Office moved, the bowling green was laid out on Butts Hill. An unwelcome change was that public houses had to shut in the afternoons and at 9 p.m. at weekends.

The war ended in November, 1918, the news welcomed with the usual bells and hooters as well as crowds in the streets who 'gave vent to their feelings in a remarkable way'. A calvery was erected to the war dead at St. John's in 1920 but the town wanted a more elaborate memorial which was to cost £5000. T.H. Woodland, the chairman of the Urban District Council (after whom Woodland Road is named), led the campaign. A plan for a town hall was abandoned in favour of a Memorial Hall. South Hill, one of Frome's great houses, was demolished to make way for it. The original design by a local architect P.B. Rigg was highly decorative but the money for it could not be raised. The resulting compromise was the austere but commodious building which was was opened by General Sir Ian Hamilton in April, 1925.

There had been no Cheese Show during the war. It was revived in 1919 and moved to a new site at Fromefield in 1920 where it was to remain until 1998. The move marked the golden jubilee of the Show which fell in 1921. Getting to the Show was facilitated in 1925 by the cutting of a new road between Wallbridge and Rodden Lake so avoiding going up and down Styles Hill. It is still called the 'New Road' causing confusion to those who expect new to mean new, but it is recent by the yardsticks of the New Forest (1100) or even New Street in Mells (1490).

Concern at the loss of ancient buildings was voiced by *'The Somerset Standard'* as early as 1927 when the Gorehedge cottages came down. Much of Palmer Street was demolished in 1923 to make way for the Co-op, Hall House in Cork Street and the fine Georgian building which housed the International Stores in the 1930s. A serious interest began to be taken in the history of Frome, first by Prebendary Daniel, then by J.O. Lewis.

Lewis was a pork butcher whose grandfather had come over from South Wales in 1815 and started with a stall in the Market Place. Local history became his hobby and he unearthed masses of material used in pamphlets, articles in the *'Standard'*, and talks to Rotary and other organisations. He died in 1947 leaving a vast 'History of Frome' in typescript which has never been published. A natural history society, the Frome-Selwood Field Club, had been started in 1919.

Between the wars Frome was still very much a country town with a population of 10,739 in 1931. Cattle were driven into market as in the old droving days. Many families kept a pig. There was a blacksmith in Christchurch Street East. Many shops kept errand boys who used 'hercules' bicycles but other deliveries were still horsedrawn. Youngsters amused themselves at the Palace or Grand Cinemas, stamping their feet for the film heroes. Otherwise there was Vallis Vale for rock climbing, swimming, bird nesting and brewing up.

For older people the crystal set and 'wireless' came in, pioneered by Frederick Cannon, in Christchurch Street East. The band played in the park on Sundays with an old WWI tank for company. Frome Town Football Club was well supported and rewarded its fans by winning the Somerset Senior Cup in 1932-33. Brewery workers received a gallon of ale a day to celebrate such occasions. There were tragedies too as when, in 1932, a footbridge over the Frome at Willow Vale collapsed drowning three boys who were on it, an event still remembered.

Industrially the big event of the inter-war period was the merger of the Art Foundry at Singers with the Morris Art Bronze factory at Lambeth in 1927 to form the firm of Singer Morris. The brass pressing side of the business remained in Frome. Despite the coming of new firms such as Nott's Industries from Swansea, there was much hardship and unemployment during the years of the Depression and long queues at the Labour Exchanges.

Politics impinged on the local scene from time to time. Mrs. Mavis Tate stood as a National Conservative in 1935. Women MPs were a novelty then but she was elected and became much liked and respected. 'Don't be late, vote for Tate' was the cry. Likewise the abdication of Edward VIII in 1936 gave rise to the ditty, appropriate for December 'Hark the herald angels sing, Mrs Simpson's pinched our king'.

Although the population was static, many people had better houses and Berkley and Rodden Roads, Windsor Crescent and Beechwood Avenue were largely developed in the 1930s. There were new schools, too. The Bluecoat School had closed in 1921 and what was to become Frome Grammar School, now the Community College, opened at Northcote House. In 1932, St. John's Senior School was built in Christchurch Street East and six years later the building of Oakfield School began to accommodate the senior classes from Milk Street.

The importance of Frome Station was diminished in 1931-32 by the creation of the loop line between Blatchbridge and Clink. Formerly, people had changed at Frome for Westbury and not the other way round and many expresses had stopped there. Watching the line being built was a great event and hundreds went up to Clink at weekends to watch.

In September, 1939, the second World War broke out and Frome geared itself to battle once more. The first evidence of the national emergency was the arrival of evacuees at Frome Station. They trooped down Vicarage Street in what seemed an endless stream to a collecting point in the Market Place. As a halfway house there was a canteen in St. John's Hall. Some of the refugees were found billets by Mr. Evemy at Mells. They arrived in time to met Queen Mary who was visiting Lady Horner from her temporary home at Badminton. The evacuees gave her three hearty cheers.

St. John's Hall did its bit for the war effort serving as a dormitory for engineering workers who took over the Selwood Printing Works and later as a canteen and recreation centre for troops. The Vicarage, too, became a rest centre for the military. Frome became a garrison town; troops took over the Keyford Tannery and The White House later Mendip Lodge Hotel, recently demolished, while there were many military camps in the vicinity. Nissen huts mushroomed. Marston House was requisitioned and visited by Queen Mary in a maroon Rolls-Royce.

Coping with British troops was one thing; the arrival of Americans added a new and lively dimension. Gérard LaRoche, who was stationed at Marston and met his future wife Joyce at a dance there, well remembers arriving at Frome's 'quaint' station on his way to help train and process American troops. One of his duties was to patrol the public houses with an English 'bobby'. This was to enforce good behaviour and segregation, black and white troops going out on different evenings. The Marston Lodge was used as a military lockup.

The 256th Engineer Battalion were unimpressed by the 'rolling, damp, rockfenced terrain'. They took to fish and chips served with dried up garden peas and ersatz juice. The Red Cross 'Doughnut Dugout' was enjoyed as were the 'movies' often seen through a haze of cigarette smoke. LaRoche also acquired a taste for fish and chips and came to think of Frome as 'a dream posting'. In 1993, Corporal Guy Stevenson presented Mrs. A. Yeoman with a plaque expressing his gratitude for the hospitality of Marston House during the war.

Bristol and Bath were heavily bombed. Children, taking advantage of high points, used to enjoy innocently the glow in the sky in the aftermath of German raids. Odd bombs were jettisoned over the countryside and such sequestered places as Buckland Dinham and Witham Friary were hit. Unbeknown to the people of Frome an important soldier took up his residence in their midst. The future Field-Marshal Viscount Montgomery of Alamein had his headquarters at the Portway Hotel in 1940. Part of the invasion of Europe was planned there as a plaque records.

Finally, in 1945, the Second World War came to an end. Frome expressed its joy and relief. The struggle had been long, costly, and exhausting but illuminated locally by a common spirit, a unity of purpose and a will to win. After the euphoria, Frome braced itself to tackle the problems of peace with austerity.

ABOVE: As if it had never been: the site of Sheppard's great factory at Spring Gardens in 1965. (FM) BELOW: Wallbridge Mills and the Maltings from the air. The massive buildings of the Maltings were taken down in the late 1960s.

ABOVE: Staff and pupils of Keyford College c1890. (FM) LEFT: The ninth Earl of Cork and Orrery was influential in Frome. RIGHT: Weymouth Road, developed in the 1890s. (FM) BELOW: Carnival procession in Christchurch Street West in the early 20th century.

ABOVE: Building workers from the firm of Seward at Mells Park House.
BELOW: Stubbs' delivery trap in action c1900. Stubbs was a butcher in Cheap Street. (FM)

ABOVE: Frome in 1905. A photograph taken from the now vanished chimney of the Electricity Works, (FM) and BELOW: the National School and Lamb Brewery buildings. (FM)

ABOVE: The Drawing Room at Wallbridge House c1880. (FM) LEFT. Keyford Grocery Stores. (FM) RIGHT: Rev W.F.H. Randolph: vicar of Frome for nearly 40 years. (FM)

ABOVE: The design for the Memorial Hall which proved too expensive for Frome. (FM) LEFT: A performing bear in Christchurch Street West in 1898. (FM) RIGHT: A link with the past revived: Mrs G.H. Boyle unveils a plaque in memory of Rev Richard Boyle and his wife E.V.B. on 1 May 1977. From the left: G.H. Boyle, R.D. Goodall, Mrs G.H. Boyle with Victoria McGarvie, Michael McGarvie, L.V. Bowring and N.F. Maggs. (SS) BELOW: Severe floods in the 1930s—one of the hazards of living in the Market Place.

Reflecting the sturdy spirit of the town: an unknown Frome lady sweeps by now demolished houses in Vicarage Street. (T)

From Past to Present

Frome marked VE Day with style. The Prime Minister's announcement of the end of the war was relayed to a large crowd in the Market Place from Woodmancy's store. An American G.I. played 'Tipperary' on a trumpet. Public buildings were illuminated that night and 10,000 boisterous people roamed the streets. There was an outbreak of street parties. Five thousand people attended a celebration in Victoria Park, spoilt by rain.

Many remember the difficult post-war years of rationing and controls. Frome was led through this testing period by Mr. H.M. Scott, Chairman of the Urban District Council. The town felt the pinch immediately as the demand for war materials slackened such as the Carley floats of which Nott's had produced more than 11,000 during the war. Nott's diversified into pressings. A more serious casualty was Houstons which closed in 1945 after having made West of England cloth in Frome since 1833.

Its Vallis Mills were taken over by Wallington Weston which had been making rubber products at Adderwell since 1897 and were now expanding into plastics. The firm, later associated with Marley, traded from the site under the name of Weston Hyde.

There was a desperate shortage of housing (which could be built only under licence.) Britain had a Labour Government but was still deeply conservative. Changing attitudes, however, are reflected in the building of the first Council housing in St. John's Road, and in the vote on Sunday opening for cinemas, a liberal measure supported overwhelmingly by Frome people. More of the old order crumbled with the death of the Marquess of Bath in 1946, followed by the sale of 24,500 acres of the Longleat Estate, mostly in the Woodlands. To the many shortages a penance was added in the bitter winter of 1947, followed by floods. During these a football match between Witham and Trudoxhill was played ankle deep in water. In the circumstances, the halves were limited to 20 minutes each.

A bright spot during these years was the revival of Frome Show after its war-time closure under the urbane Presidency of Arthur Duckworth, of Orchardleigh. There were still classes for cottagers and smallholders, for cart horses and for thatching ricks.

Just as the post-war restrictions were easing and life was returning to normal, came the death of King George VI in 1952. This was a shock. Flags flew at half mast, the Grand and Gaumont cinemas closed, and the Librarian, Hedley Pudden, wrote a poem extolling the King's virtues:

In ways of humbleness and right
the path of duty daily trod;
Virtuous in his Kingly flight,
He renders up his crown to God.

A fanfare played by three trumpeters of the Town Band preceded the proclamation of Queen Elizabeth II by Mr. H.M. Scott from the steps of the Public Offices. The crowd was estimated at 400 or less, a falling off from the great gatherings of the past. The Elizabethan age had begun.

A new reign was marked by a grant to Frome by the College of Arms of its own armorial bearings. An unofficial coat-of-arms had been used for 50 years and turns up on old pieces of Goss pottery. The position was now legalised, the Arms featuring a teazel for the woollen industry, an ermined chevron, which had been borne by the Leversedge family, and two sallow trees representing Selwood Forest.

The griffin supporters were dropped as was the sheep crest, taken from the Arms of the Sheppard family. Instead we have a demidragon holding a crozier and emerging from a Saxon crown. This symbolises Frome's links with the Saxon kings and with St. Aldhelm and Cirencester Abbey.

In July, 1955, Mrs. Katharine Ashworth, who was educated in Frome and had family connections with the town, wrote a fine article called 'Memories of Frome' for 'Country Life' which powerfully evokes the spirit of the place in her day. She found it 'a busy industrial town and the manufacture of cloth persists side by side with new industries which have taken the place of the old - gloves, plastic, metal works, life floats and a large modern creamery. The Cheese Show, the second largest in Britain, continues to flourish....'

She wrote of its secret charms so often missed by passing motorists (as is still true today) 'steep and narrow streets, many of them cobbled, lined with old houses, bow windows, gables and carved wooden balconies. Here solid merchants' houses, two roomed cottages, ancient smoky taverns and a chapel or two with a factory jammed between, all jostle for positions, each from necessity holding up its neighbour'.

The same year that Mrs. Ashworth was gathering material for her perceptive account of Frome, Miss le Gros, of the family which had owned the silk mills in Merchants Barton, died. Her home, North Hill House, was bought by the Urban District Council. This enabled it to move out of the Public Offices and into its own headquarters.

On the whole the 1950s and 1960s were active and prosperous years. It is true that some of the old-established industries disappeared: Cockey's, ironfounders, were taken over by Matbro in 1960 and the last cloth factory, Tucker's of Wallbridge, closed in 1965, breaking Frome's long association with clothmaking. The mill became a carpet factory but coats of heavy West of England cloth made there are still being worn today. Another loss was S. Rawlings & Son, makers of cards and belting, which was reputed to have been in business for 250 years.

Butler & Tanner, Singer's and smaller firms, such as the Somerset Smithy, remained and Frome's light industrial base was broadened by the arrival of newcomers such as John Wallis Titt in 1955 and Cuprinol 10 years later. With the population growing and the danger of Frome becoming a dormitory town for Bath and Bristol clearly perceived, there was a drive to find new employers. Many firms established themselves on the newly formed Marston Trading Estate.

As we have seen quarrying was an ancient local occupation. It now became more dominant with the extension of the Whatley quarry by ARC (now Hanson) and the opening of Foster Yeoman's Torr works at East Cranmore in 1964. These became two of the largest quarries in Europe.

Amid these commercial concerns there was a growing interest in the history of the town and concern about the disappearance of its ancient buildings. In 1956, the Keyford Asylum, one of Frome's most distinctive buildings, was demolished to the regret of many. Two years later at a meeting at the house of Mr. Hilary Daniel, a solicitor, it was decided to form the Frome Society for Local Study. Mr. Daniel went on to become a leading townsman, a stalwart of a multitude of good causes touching most aspects of local life.

Mr. J.C. Hughes, Clerk of the Rural District Council, was the first Chairman of the Society. The foundations of its future success were laid by Mrs. H.M. Massey and Eunice Overend. Under their direction it was exceedingly active and with the support of the Urban and Rural Councils, opened a museum at the Old Church House in 1966. It was intended 'to appeal to the casual visitor and to those who wanted to see objects displayed and to do research'.

There was plenty of recording for the Society to do. Conservation was not yet fashionable. The Urban Council was bent on demolishing old slums and replacing them with decent modern housing, a worthy objective, although some of the new designs were themselves the height of indecency. In the early 1960s many of the 17th and 18th century houses in the Trinity area were swept away, although, to its credit, the council repaired some of the houses in Trinity Street and retained them.

The north side of Broadway was taken down including the United Brewery to be replaced by the Dorset Close housing development. The west side of Bridge Street was demolished, and later, the charming, though derelict, houses of Gorehedge, together with the old Lamb Brewery. It was difficult to find uses for other buildings which were in a poor state of repair. The National School in Bath Street was decaying. Rook Lane Chapel had been abandoned by its congregation who had settled at Zion (now the Zion United Reformed Church) and the future of one of the finest nonconformist chapels in the West of England became uncertain.

Even the Blue House was threatened. The Council was prepared to see it demolished but Frome people rallied to its defence. As the result of an appeal led by Mr. D.G.E. Beswick, the building was restored in 1965, a signal of success in a bleak period. John Betjeman considered it a triumph, a tribute to Frome's foresight and to its heart.

Although the population of Frome was still only 12530 in 1970, the town began its phenomenal expansion in the early 1960s. More than 1000 Council houses were built, especially in the northeast part of Frome around Monmouth Drive and in the south-west, Stourton View and its satellites. The trend was accelerated when in 1969 the County Council decided that Frome should be an area of concentrated urban expansion with a population limit of 25,000. A catchment area allowed for another 10,000 people. The aim was to prevent the further growth of Bristol and Bath and the destruction of the green belt.

The private sector now became involved in the bonanza and the Critchill Estate emerged between 1969 and 1975 as well as the Mendip Drive development opposite the grammar school. This later extended into Packsaddle. The pressure to build has not abated despite the enormous number of houses erected and the lack of new facilities or employment opportunities. There are few brown field sites left to fill, almost every space, suitable or unsuitable, being earmarked for development. The choice of green field sites arouses general concern and passionate local opposition.

The dominant topic in Frome in the 1970s was conservation. 'Here is the puzzle about Frome', wrote Gavin Stamp,' that so fine and interesting a West Country town should have been so badly treated by its authorities'. Many shared this view including Mr. R.D. Goodall, a young architect, who gave voice to the widely felt indignation about the destruction of so many ancient buildings. In 1971, Mr. Goodall was instrumental in founding the Civic Society and an Historic Buildings Trust was set up under the chairmanship of Mr. Arthur Sutton. It helped restore buildings in Vicarage Street and Vallis Way.

The Frome Society was also active in this cause led by Mr. L.V. Bowring and his wife Phyllis. Mr. Bowring began his long chairmanship, which lasted until 1997, in 1971. In particular, the Society fought a vigorous campaign to save Marston House from demolition in 1972, a successful undertaking strongly supported by 'The Somerset Standard'. The same

147

year, the Frome Society published the first serious history of the town, 'The Making of Frome', by Peter Belham, an economic historian who was deputy head of the grammar school.

The debates over Council plans to demolish the remainder of the Trinity area as well as Badcox Lane Chapel and its handsome classical portico, houses at Vallis Way, the future of Rook Lane Chapel, and various road schemes, were passionate and strongly argued. Generally the Council - and especially the chairman of planning, George Coleman - were unsympathetic to conservation, although the conservationists had a devoted, if ponderous, ally in Mr. N.F. Maggs. The historian Peter Belham was chairman of the council; skilful and judicious, he strove to be fair to both parties.

The various controversies were well covered by the media, even television, and 'The Somerset Standard' under editor Jack Wheeler, who was interested in history and who liked Frome, devoted many columns to the subject. Its reporter was Jack Perry, a former editor, known as 'Mr. Frome', a man much liked who seemed to know everyone and everything. A lively element in the debate was the 'Save Trinity' group, who, although small in number attracted much attention.

In January, 1974, the Council invited the general public to an open meeting at North Hill House to discuss conservation issues. This can now be seen as the event where the tide turned in favour of conservation. The meeting was packed and many were turned away. Few who were present at this airing of grievances will ever forget it. Conservation did not immediately become easy but the philistines saw the writing on the wall.

By this time the Urban District Council, which had ruled Frome since 1894, was about to join the manorial courts and the Local Board as part of history. It went out amid a flurry of activity. One of its last acts was the creation of the Westway Shopping Precinct. Brick built and utilitarian, it was architecturally unexciting but well integrated into the town centre. In recent years its harsh lines have been softened with a neo-Georgian gloss.

Kingsway, which contained Safeway, Frome's introduction to supermarket shopping, and other retail outlets, was in the pipeline. Its construction together with Saxonvale and its carpark, entailed the destruction of the Iron Gates gardens.

A new secondary modern school, Selwood, had been opened in Berkley Road in 1958 to replace the over-crowded St. John's School. Selwood was described as 'a magnificent new building set in over 14 acres of school estate, with fine playing fields and all the advantages that a newly equipped school can offer'. Now, with the introduction of a tertiary system of education, the old grammar school was transformed into a community college on the comprehensive model. Both the Urban and Rural Councils co-operated to provide a Sports (Leisure) Centre and a theatre (Merlin), admirable new amenities for the growing town whose population reached 16,000 in 1975.

There was much misgiving about local government re-organisation. Many hoped that the Urban and Rural Districts might merely be amalgamated. Others thought Frome would be out on a limb in the large new authority and considered that Frome lay naturally with the Wiltshire towns of Warminster, Westbury and Trowbridge. But Somerset loyalties prevailed. The 80 year rule of the Urban Council was celebrated with a civic exhibition and a 'community year' of events and displays.

Frome became part of Mendip District in 1974, surrendering power for dignity being given a Mayor. A veterinary surgeon, Peter Bardgett, was the first to hold the office. The new Mendip Council did not at first prove as sympathetic to conservation as had been hoped. Some new councillors were, of course, old councillors wearing a different hat. Gradually, Frome's unique quality as a surviving ancient wool town came to be recognised. This was underlined by the creation of a wide Conservation Area and by the Listing of more and more of its buildings as of architectural or historic interest.

Mendip District Council were persuaded to restore what remained of the Trinity area and more than 100 houses were repaired or rebuilt according to a sympathetic plan proposed by Moxley, Jenner and Partners. The Trinity area now provides good homes, attracts discerning visitors and is generally a credit to the town. Badcox Lane Chapel was saved as were the old houses in Vallis Way (in 1985), the new road being routed around them instead of through them.

The restoration of Marston House by Foster Yeoman in 1984-1990 as its headquarters gave Frome a venue for many events and charitable occasions the like of which it had never had before. Sun Street, once scheduled for demolition, was transformed from ruin to pleasantness and charm. The perennial problem of Rook Lane Chapel was partially solved by the Somerset Building Preservation Trust in 1993. They thoroughly repaired the building. Community and office use were proposed in 2001.

The early 1980s were another difficult period of recession and unemployment. A positive and memorable event was the celebration in 1985 of 1300 years of Frome's existence since its foundation by St. Aldhelm. The head of the Sheppard family, the cricketing Bishop of Liverpool, preached at a thanksgiving service at St. John's. A window was commissioned from Mark Angus illustrating Frome's long history in a symbolic way.

The last decade is almost too close to judge or even record. The year of the by-pass, much heralded, came in 1989. It improved Frome's road system but did little to relieve congestion in the town centre. Two years later Frome became home to an imaginative monumental complex, ECOS, the European Community of Stones, created by sculptor Barry Cooper. It consists of an amphitheatre surrounded by monoliths from nine EEC countries, a remarkable edifice to find in a country town.

Frome continued to grow especially along Berkley Road and The Piggeries were cleared and redeveloped by Mendip with flair. The population is thought to have reached 23,000. The Blue House was twice restored and improved and visited by the Prince of Wales in 1995. Nevertheless, the decade was one of marking time, of missed opportunities, of negative developments.

The cattle market moved out to Standerwick in 1990 to be followed by the show nine years later; good moves no doubt for the organisations concerned but bad news for the town. All attempts to develop the old cattle market as a shopping or civic complex ran into the ground. The coming of Sainsbury's may have enhanced Frome's shopping facilities but it has also put pressure on small businesses and drawn trade away from the town centre.

We may be in a period of drift, but positive elements remain: despite vandalism, dirt, congestion, occasional violence (which have always been with us) Frome is a genuine and friendly place, gregarious and generous, a good place to live. It is curious, an industrial town set in beautiful countryside, unchanging despite its enlargement, absorbing newcomers without surrendering its traditional characteristics, it is too sensible to be given to great enthusiasm and is not inclined to wear its heart on its sleeve. Taking a survey of 1000 years, one is struck by the continuity of families and institutions, the changeless framework of local life and the evergreen resilience of the town and its people.

So, as Shakespeare writes in 'Henry V' :
Thus far with rough and all unable pen,
Our bending author hath pursued the story
In little room confining mighty men,
Mangling by starts the full course of their glory

Bibliography

This book is to some extent based on manuscript material, much of it at Frome Museum and in possession of the Historical Research Group, more from other sources. The chief printed sources are given below

Adams, David L. *Frome's Fallen Heroes,* 2000

Ashworth, Mrs K. *Memories of Frome* Country Life, 21 July, 1955

Bede, The Venerable *The Ecclesiastical History of the English Nation,* Everyman's Library, 1930

Bates, E.H. *Leland in Somersetshire,* Proc Som Arch Soc, 33, 1887. *The Black Death in Somerset,* Proc Som Arch Soc, 63, 1917

Belham, P. *The Making Of Frome,* FSLS, 1973
St. Aldhelm and the Founding of Frome, Frome 1300 Publications, 1985
Villages of the Frome Area, FSLS, 1992

Bennett, Rev W.J.E. *The Old Church of St John of Froome,* Penny, 1866

The Blue House Restored, 1965

Bowden, Samuel *Poems on various subjects,* 1754

Browne, Bishop G.F., *St Aldhelm: His life and Times,* 1903

Bunn, Thomas *A Letter relative to... the affairs of Frome Selwood,* 1834. *Answers to Inquiries respecting Frome Selwood,* 1851

Burnett, David *Longleat,* 1978

Burrow, E.J. *Ancient Earthworks and Camps of Somerset,* 1924

Calendar of Patent Rolls Calendar of Close Rolls

Calendar of the Committee for the Advance of Money Calendar of Charter Rolls

Calendar of the Committee for Compounding

Calendar of Inquisitions Post Mortem

Cleverdon, Rev F.W. ed. McGarvie *A History of Mells,* FSLS, 1974 reprinted 2003

Cockey, L.S. *The Cockeys of the West Country,* Somerset Standard, 6 August 1954

Coles, J. *Frome at the end of the 18th Century,* Frome Almanack, 1936

Cook, G.H. *Mediaeval Chantries and Chantry Chapels,* 1947

Court, A. *Fifty Years of Farming,* Frome 1300 Publications, 1985

Cuzner, Samuel *Handbook to Froome-Selwood,* 1866

Daniel, Rev W.E. *The Street Names of Frome* and *Frome in the 16th Century,* pamphlet, various editions

Daniel, Rev W.E. *History of the priests who have served the Church of Froome,* St John's Parish Magazine, 1886

Darby, H.C. and R. Welldon Finn *Domesday Geography of South West England,* 1967

Day, J.K. *Rodden Church, Frome,* 2001

Dix, R. *Looking Back on Frome,* Somerset Standard, 1 January, 1932

Dobson, DP. *The Archaeology of Somerset,* 1931

Douie, D.L. and Farmer, H. *Magna Viti Sancti Hugonis,* 1961/62

Dunning, R.W. *Christianity in Somerset,* 1976.
History of Somerset, Somerset County Library, 1978 Reprinted 1987

Eden, Sir Frederick *The State of the Poor,* 1938

Ekwall, E. *Oxford Dictionary of English Place-Names,* 1936

Finn, R. Welldon *Domesday Book: A Guide,* 1973

Frome Almanack, various dates between 1878 and 1939

Frome and District Agricultural Society *Frome Cheese Show Centenary, 1877-1977,* Programme

Frome Official Guide, 1980 edition

Gentleman's Magazine Library *Topographical History of Shropshire and Somersetshire,* 1898

Gill, D.J. *The story of Christ Church, Frome* (n.d)
Frome School Days Frome 1300 Publications, 1985
The Sheppards and Eighteenth Century Frome, FSLS, 1982
Selwood, Selwood School Parent/Staff Association, 1983
Bath Street, privately printed, 1990
Britain in Old Photographs: Frome, Sutton, 1995

Goodall,R.D. *The Buildings of Frome* Frome 1300 Publications, 1985

Grundy, G.B. *The Saxon Charters of Somerset,* 1935

Harvey, John *Sources for the History of Houses,* 1974.
The Manors of Orchardleigh, Egford and Egforton, Notes and Queries for Somerset and Dorset, XXXI, 1980

Harvey, W.J. *The story of Zion Congregational Chapel, Frome,* 1918

H.M.S.O., *Early Industrial Housing: The Trinity Area of Frome,* 1981

Hylton, Lord *The Manor Houses of Hardington and Vallis,* Proc Som Arch Soc, 74, 1928

Hughes, H.S. *The Gentle Hertford: Her Life and Letters,* 1940

Jackson, Canon J-E. *Charles, Lord Stourton and the Murder of the Hartgills,*

1864 Kelly's *Directory of Somerset,* 1861, 1875, 1883

Lewis, J.O. *Notes for the History of Frome,* Proc Som Arch Soc, 78, 1932.
Frome Charities, Somerset Standard, April, 1932.
Early Nonconformity in Frome, pamphlet.
Frome's Early History, Frome Almanack, 1934.
Frome in the Early Part of the 19th century, Frome Almanack, 1929

Major, A.F. *The Early Wars of Wessex,* 1913

Malmesbury, William of *Gesta Pontificum Anglorum,* 1870

Maton, W.G. *Observations relative to... the West Country of England,* 1797

Margary, I.D. *Roman Roads in Britain,* 1967

McGarvie, Michael *Eighty Years of Frome,* 1974 (contains important articles by A.W. Hodder and R.D. Goodall). *Light in Selwood, FSLS* 1976.
The Bounds of Selwood, FSLS, 1979.
Argyll House, FSLS, 1980.
Diaries tell of a Frome Courtship in Georgian Days (Thomas Green), 23 March, 1973
Once Famous, now she is forgotten (Elizabeth Rowe), 6 September, 1974
Source of the River Frome 8 August 1975   Somerset
The Faces of the Past 23 April 1976   Standard
The story of Robert Porteous, founder of Frome Cheese Show 12 August 1977
Just where was the Chapel of St Katherine? 10 February 1978
Portraits give a glimpse into Frome's Past 15 February, 1980

Frome in Old Picture Postcards, European Library, 3 volumes, 1983-85
Around Frome, Chalford, 1997
The Book of Marston Bigot, Barracuda/Yeoman, 1987
Frome Place-Names, FSLS, *1983,* reprinted 1992
Crime and Punishment in Regency Frome, FSLS, 1984
Frome through the Ages, FSLS, 1982, reprinted 2000
Frome Society Year Books, 1-13, 1987-2009
The Story of the Grange, Tytherington, 1992

Massey, G.*The Bells of Frome Deanery,* Frome 1300 Publications 1985

Moxley, Jenner and Partners, *A Report on the Future of the Trinity Area of Frome* 1977

Olive, John *Notes on Shawford Mill,* 1977

Overend, E *The Geology of Frome Area,* Frome 1300 Publications 1985

Partridge, Ann *Frome Selwood,* Somerset and Wessex Life, June 1973

Pearman, A. *Sheppard's Plaid,* Somerset Standard, 19 May, 1950

Pevsner, Nikolaus *North Somerset and Bristol* (Penguin Buildings of England Series), 1958

Pococke, Dr Richard *Travels through England,* 1889

Ponting, K.G. *The Woollen Industry of South-West England,* Adams and Dart 1971. *Wool and Water,* Moonraker Press 1975

Porter, H.M. *The Saxon Conquest of Somerset and Devon,* 1967. *St Aldhelm: Abbot and Bishop,* 1978. *St. Aldhelm,* FSLS, 1984

Richardson, John *The Local Historians Encyclopaedia,* 1974

Rogers, K. *Wiltshire and Somerset Woollen Mills,* 1976

Rook Lane Chapel *Bi-centenary Celebrations,* Somerset and Wilts Journal, 4 October, 1907

Ross, C.D. *The Cartulary of Cirencester Abbey,* first two volumes, 1964

Rotary Club of Frome, *Frome: A Special Town,* 1995

Rotary Club of Frome Selwood, *Frome Past and Present, 1999*

Rowe, Mrs Elizabeth *Poetical Works,* cl808

Russell, G. *Frome then and now,* Frome 1300 Publications 1985

Somerset Archaeological Society Proceedings 1849-

Somerset and Dorset Notes and Queries, 1894-

Somerset Record Society 1887-

Somerset and Wilts Journal *Jubilee Supplement,* 7 July, 1905

Stecher, H.F. *Elizabeth Singer Rowe, The Poetess of Frome,* 1973

Taylor, Christopher *Fields in the English Landscape,* 1975

Thompson, E.H. *Forest Pleas, Somerset: Selwood,* SDNQ V, 1897; VI 1895. *Frome Mediaeval Charters,* SDNQ VII, 1901. *Branch family Charters,* SDNQ, IX, 1905

Timperley, H.W. & Brill, Edith *The Ancient Trackways of Wessex,* 1965

Tuck, S. *Wesleyan Methodism in Frome,* 1837

Tuck, Mrs *Vallis Vale, and other poems,* 1823

Twelvetrees, D. *The Future of the Past,* FSLS, 1974

Underdown, David *Somerset in the Civil War and Interregnum,* 1973

Victoria History of the County of Somerset, volumes 1 and 2

Warner, Richard *Excursions from Bath*, 1801

Weaver, Rev F.W. *Somerset Incumbents,* 1889

Wesley, Rev John *Journal,* 4 volumes, Everyman's Library

Woodeforde, Rev C. *Stained Glass in Somerset*, 1946

Ziegler, Philip *The Black Death,* 1969

Additional Bibliography

Bunn, Thomas *Experiences of a 19th Century Gentleman Gill, D.J.,* FSLS, 2003

Gill, D.J. and Buckley, J.W.H. *Willow Vale Frome,* FSLS, 2010

Goodall, R.D. *The Buildings of Frome,* 2nd Edition, FSLS, 2004 3rd Edition FSLS, 2013
    The Industries of Frome, FSLS, 2009

Green, Hilary, *Around Frome,* Frith, 2001

Perry, G.S. *The Coopers' Company's School in Frome 1939-1945,* 2006

OS 1886 map of Frome, FSLS, 2011

OS 1903 Map of Frome, FSLS, 2007

Thornes, R. *Men of Iron, The Fussells of Mells,* FSLS, 2010

Windrum, Anthony *The History of Nunney,* FSLS, 1998, reprinted 2008

Index

156

158

162